Klaus Fuchs

The Man Who Stole the Atom Bomb

NORMAN MOSS

First published in Great Britain by Grafton Books in 1987.

This edition published by Sharpe Books in 2018.

ISBN: 9781790794041

Other Books by Norman Moss

Men Who Play God: the Story of the Hydrogen Bomb
A British/American Dictionary
The Pleasures of Deception
The Politics of Uranium

CONTENTS

CHAPTER ONE

In the spring of 1942 the war in Russia was nearing the end of its first year. The savage Russian resistance and the equally savage Russian winter had dashed Hitler's hopes of a quick blitzkrieg victory over the Soviet Union to follow those in the West, and littered the landscape with the frozen wrecks of thousands of German tanks, trucks and artillery pieces, and the frozen bodies of tens of thousands of German soldiers. The invaders were being pushed back from the approaches to Moscow, and war was raging along a 4,500-mile front. Now Soviet armies were girding themselves to meet the next German offensive, and the Soviet Government was mobilizing industry and population for a prolonged and bitter struggle that would tax the nation's resources to the utmost.

One day in April, the Soviet Foreign Minister, Vyacheslav Molotov, called the Minister for the Chemical Industry, Mikhail Pervukhin, into his office. He handed Pervukhin a file containing intelligence reports of work that was going on in secret in Western countries on a new kind of weapon, a uranium bomb, that would explode by releasing the energy locked inside the atom. Molotov said he was giving him this file on the instructions of Stalin himself. He told Pervukhin to consult scientists knowledgeable in this field, and determine what action, if any, should be taken in the light of these reports.

Pervukhin did so. Soviet atomic physicists, like their counterparts elsewhere, were aware by now that the creation of an explosion by atomic fission was theoretically possible. The reports in this file showed that it was a practical possibility as well. The scientists gave their advice, and Pervukhin reported to Stalin. Within months a laboratory was

1

set up to work on atomic fission, scientists were taken off other war work to staff it, and the Soviet atomic bomb programme was under way.

The principal contributor to these files, sending back reports via a Soviet agent in Britain, was a pale, bespectacled, unusually taciturn physicist who had been brought up always to do what his conscience told him to, Klaus Fuchs.

A little while after this, in the summer of 1944, on a Saturday afternoon, Klaus Fuchs was driving through Santa Fe, New Mexico. He had on the seat beside him a large envelope containing data on the atomic bomb that was being built in secret at Los Alamos, some thirty miles from the city. This project was the best-kept secret of the war, and the most important secret in the world. But the envelope he had with him was a virtual information pack on the bomb, containing descriptions, calculations, figures, and even a scale drawing.

Fuchs stopped the car on an avenue with overhanging trees that provided some shade from the burning southwestern sun, and looked around for a familiar figure. He saw him almost at once, a medium-built, pudgy-faced man with thick glasses. The man got into the car, and Fuchs drove a short distance and parked, and the two of them talked. Then Fuchs handed the man the envelope; the latter got out and walked away, and Fuchs drove off. The man went to the bus station, to wait for the next bus to Albuquerque, where he was to make a call the next day on a US army sergeant.

***

If ever a man was his father's son, it was Klaus Fuchs. This is not to say that he was just like his father, for they followed very different careers, and Fuchs senior had some qualities which his son Klaus conspicuously lacked. But the mainsprings of Klaus Fuchs's action can be seen in his father's life and deepest beliefs.

Emil Fuchs was a clergyman in the Lutheran Church, the

church that claims direct descent from the man who most effectively raised the banner of individual conscience against the claims to spiritual authority of the Roman Catholic Church. Indeed, the principles that Klaus Fuchs followed, and his justification to himself for betraying his oath of allegiance to his adopted country, can be traced right back to Martin Luther's famous statement of defiance to the Diet of Worms in 1521: 'I do not accept the authority of popes and councils... My conscience is captive to the word of God.'

The mainstream of the Lutheran Church has always taken good care to render unto Caesar the things that are Caesar's; it has accepted the temporal authority of the state, as Luther himself did, and has tended to be conservative. Emil Fuchs was one of a radical minority, ready to challenge injustices perpetrated by the state in the name of Christian values. He was a Socialist for most of his life, and a brave opponent of Nazism.

Like Luther, like the heroes of Protestantism, he was ready to follow the dictates of his conscience whatever others said, and whatever the consequences. His moral priorities are seen in a passage in a pamphlet he wrote, *Christ in Catastrophe,* recalling some of his fears as the father of a family during the early Hitler years: 'People who fell into Nazi hands were treated with great cruelty, and I was in great anxiety. One night I nearly went mad. I saw my children cruelly killed, lying before me, and in this hour of utter despair, I heard a voice saying: "What do you want? Shall they keep their lives by losing their conscience?" Peace came to me.'

His religious beliefs changed during the course of his life. He wrote later of 'spiritual struggle', and 'wrestling with questions'. This kind of travail is inherent in the Protestant doctrine, and accounts of tormenting inner struggles run through the writings of the great figures of Protestantism, including Luther himself. For if one has to find the answer to moral and spiritual questions in oneself rather than in any outside authority, it is sometimes difficult to distinguish the voice of God from that of the Devil, of true morality from proud error. A battle rages inside the head. It raged inside his, and it was to rage inside his son's.

As a young clergyman, Emil Fuchs went to Manchester to be the pastor to a German congregation there, and he learned to speak English. He became concerned at the condition of industrial workers in city slums, and he retained this concern when he went back to Germany. He worried that his church was not doing enough to reach these people. He started weekly discussions in his home on religious and social issues, mainly for industrial workers, Christian or not, and these continued for several years. A short, tubby man, he had a warm, outgoing personality that enabled him to establish relationships with many different kinds of people.

He joined the Social Democratic Party, the SPD, in 1912, one of the few clergymen to do so. He identified Christianity with the poor and deprived, and refused to separate the Christian mission from the political struggle for social betterment, and against militarism.

Later he became a Quaker, and in the years after World War II he spent some time with Quakers in America and Britain. Some of these who met him testify to his strength of mind and the warmth of his personality, as well as the evident intensity of his faith. One man said, 'I didn't see a lot of him — I only met him a few times — but I felt I knew him. There are people you can spend ten minutes with and feel you've spent the whole day with them. Emil Fuchs was one of these.' Interestingly, people were to say precisely the opposite about his son Klaus: that they could spend days with him, and not know him at all.

Klaus Fuchs was born on 29 December 1911 in the village of Rüsselsheim, near Frankfurt, where his father was the local clergyman. He was born at the end of the twenty-eighth year of the reign of Kaiser Wilhelm II, into a stable German society that would vanish before he reached adulthood. He was christened Emil Julius Klaus Fuchs, but used only the last of his Christian names. He was the third of four children. There was an elder brother, Gerhardt, a sister Elizabeth, and then, after Klaus, a younger sister, Kristel.

His confession of espionage, written in 1950, was an autobiographical statement. Of his childhood, he wrote simply: 'My father was a parson, and I had a very happy childhood. I think that the one thing that mostly stands out is that my father always did what he believed to be the right thing to do and he always told us that we had to go our own way, even if he disagreed.'

There are two strange things about this declaration. One is the bland statement that he had not just a happy childhood, but a very happy childhood. Later events in the Fuchs family point backwards to stresses that one would expect to have cast some shadows in the home, remembered or not. The other is the nature of this recollection: the *one* thing that stands out in this supposedly very happy childhood is not a memory of love, or warmth, or joyous occasions, but a moral example and a moral precept.

He grew up in the social and political turmoil in Germany that followed the 1918 defeat, which brought with it the downfall of the monarchy and its replacement by a republic. The defeat was traumatic for a nation confident of its own superiority. Then came attempted putsches by the Left and the Right, political assassinations, and a hyper-inflation which made money worthless for a while, turned many people who had comfortable savings into embittered paupers, and left Germans with little confidence in national institutions. Moral standards became as arbitrary as political ones. The sexual activities that were the dark secrets of the Kaiser's court were flaunted. This was the Germany of Bertolt Brecht and Kurt Weill, and *The Threepenny Opera,* and Christopher Isherwood, and *Cabaret.*

But Fuchs lived his life in prose.

When he was still young, the family moved from Rüsselsheim to Eisenach, a picturesque industrial town of some 50,000 people in Thuringia, in what is now East Germany. He was an outstandingly good student. In 1928, when Eisenach decided to mark the tenth anniversary of the founding of the German republic by awarding a prize for exemplary work to a single student in the local *Gymnasium,* or high school, it was won by Fuchs. After the *Gymnasium,* he went on to study mathematics and physics at the University of Leipzig. As a child he was left-handed, and he remained left-handed in most things, but he was taught to write with his right hand.

As a teenager he was unusually sure of himself, and self-contained. The Fuchs children came in for some unpleasant remarks at school because of their father's unpopular political views; Emil noted that Gerhardt used to be upset by this, but Klaus was untroubled by the opinions of others. He did not confide in his father as much as Gerhardt did, although he admired him.

When Fuchs was nineteen, tragedy came to the family. His mother, Else, had often suffered from fits of depression. One day in October 1931, Emil came home to find her lying on the floor, dying. She had drunk hydrochloric acid, a particularly painful way of committing suicide. Her last words were, 'Mother, I'm coming.' Only after her death did Emil learn that her mother had also killed herself. Later, their eldest daughter would take her own life, making a third generation of suicides, and their other daughter would be a patient in a mental hospital in America. Klaus Fuchs hardly ever spoke of his mother in later life.

Emil Fuchs prided himself on being a liberal father and encouraging his children to form their own views, but in fact they all shared his social concerns and his left-wing orientation. They were known to some in Eisenach as 'the red foxes' — *fuchs* being the German word for 'fox'.

At Leipzig University, Fuchs joined the student branch of the Social Democratic Party, the SPD, and also the Reichsbanner, an SPD paramilitary organization formed in opposition to the Nazis' SA, the Brownshirts. In his own mind, this was a break with his father's pacifist beliefs. Fuchs was slightly built, with thin arms and legs, and he wore glasses; he showed physical courage in joining the Reichsbanner, for they sometimes had to battle with the Brownshirts in the streets. He passed out leaflets for the SPD, and spoke at student meetings. He chose his friends only from among those who shared his political inclinations.

He talked to Communist students, and found that two things set him against the Communists. One was that these students would follow the party line strictly and uncritically, even though they might disagree with it privately on some points. The other was that while the Communist Party was calling continually for united action with the Social Democrats, it was at the same time denouncing the Social Democrat leaders in violent terms.

Politics took up a great deal of his time and energy during his student days. Politics in Germany at this time was intense, and there was a great deal at stake. A person's political viewpoint was not a minor adjunct of his life, like a hobby; it was seen as central, and often determined his life-style and his friends. The issue was much more than what political party would govern. Political struggles were carried on not only within the framework of the constitution, but also around it.

Even after the post-1918 upheavals had subsided, the institutions of the German Republic that was established at Weimar did not receive anything like universal support. Several of the Republic's founding fathers had been murdered as 'traitors' because they had accepted the surrender in 1918. One section of German society wanted simply to annul these past years and restore the monarchy. There was no common ground among all the contending political parties. The political questions that confronted the citizens were about the kind of state in which they would live, and the flag their children would salute: would it have the red, black and gold bars of the flag of the Republic, or the old Imperial insignia, or a hammer and sickle, or a swastika? The country was in a state of ideological civil war. Fuchs threw himself into this struggle vigorously.

The Fuchs family moved to North Germany, to the rainy Baltic seaport of Kiel. Emil Fuchs took up an academic post, as Professor of Theology at a teachers' training college. Fuchs himself entered Kiel University.

There, he joined a student organization which included members of both the SPD and the Communist Party, and he was made Chairman. They approached Nazi students and tried to persuade them to change their ideas, for Nazism had an appeal for youthful idealism, despite its brutality, and it had an appeal also for radical social views which might otherwise find a natural outlet on the Left. The Nazi student organization at the University was campaigning for lower fees; Fuchs decided to take them at their word, and he proposed that the two groups organize jointly a student strike for reduced fees. He met the leader of the Nazi students several times in secret to negotiate on this, but the Nazi hedged.

Then he did something which earned him the bitter hostility of the Nazi student organization and gave him some private misgivings. He issued a leaflet giving an account of these discussions, and saying this showed that the Nazis were not serious in their demands for lower fees but were simply using the issue to try to gain popularity. He reflected later that it was not fair to publish an account of these secret talks without first warning the Nazis that he was going to do so, or at least giving them an ultimatum that he would go public unless they took some action. Many years later, when he wrote his

8

autobiographical confession, this still troubled him and he wrote: 'I had violated some standards of decent behaviour.' Nobody taxed him with the morality of what he did. He raised the question himself within his own mind, and answered it within his own mind, as he was to work out other moral questions later.

He broke with the SPD over the party's policy in the 1932 presidential election. The Social Democrats supported the old President, General von Hindenburg, as the alternative to Hitler, who was a rival candidate. The Communists wanted a united front of working-class parties, that is, with the Socialists, against both Hindenburg and Hitler, and Fuchs favoured this policy. When the Communist Party ran its leader, Ernst Thaelmann, as a presidential candidate, Fuchs offered to speak for him, and he was expelled from the SPD. Hindenburg won the election.

Shortly after this, the Conservative Chancellor, Franz von Papen, dismissed the elected Social Democratic Government of Prussia, the largest German state, sending in police to drag the members out of their offices. Fuchs went to the Communist Party headquarters and found old friends from the SPD Reichsbanner there, ready to take to the streets to fight for Social Democracy in Prussia, all of them turning to the party that seemed to be taking the most active role in resistance to the Right. But the Prussian Social Democrats limited their resistance to an appeal to Germany's Supreme Court.

Fuchs joined the Communist Party, accepting now the need for party discipline in the fight against Nazism. His brother Gerhardt and his sisters Elizabeth and Kristel joined in the same year. They all discussed their reasons with their father. He disagreed with their decision, but he was not entirely unsympathetic, for he also was disappointed in the Social Democratic leaders' attitude to the Nazi threat.

Fuchs was motivated, as many others were at the time, not only by fear of Nazism but also by the hope offered by Communism. It is important that in 1932 the most dramatic horrors of Soviet Communism that were seen from the West — the purges, the mass deportations — were still in the future. Arthur Koestler, who was later to analyse the Communist mentality perceptively and profoundly, joined the German Communist Party at this time, as a journalist in Berlin, and he recalled in his autobiography: 'Russia was still regarded as "the great experiment"; one could have reservations about the regime and be critical of it, but there was no *prima facie* case for rejecting it out of hand. Only the conservatives and reactionaries did that.'[i]

For a while, in the late 1920s, things had seemed to be stabilizing in Germany. But then came the Depression in America, and its repercussions in Europe. Capital was withdrawn from German industry, millions of people were thrown out of work and the economy went into decline. There were strikes, and Nazis and their opponents fought savage battles in the streets. In this time of national distress and near-despair, people sought strong leadership. When parliamentary elections were held in 1932, more people voted for the Nazi Party than for any other party, although the Nazis still did not have a majority of seats. The Social Democrats were the biggest minority party, with the Communists in next place. The following January, when another coalition government fell apart, von Papen, who had resigned as Chancellor a few months earlier, urged President Hindenburg to offer the office of Chancellor to Hitler, assuring him that these wild men of the Right would be tamed by the responsibilities of office, and Hindenburg took his advice.

Hitler became Chancellor in January 1933 with a coalition cabinet, including members of other parties, and the democratic institutions remained in existence. But if these had seemed shaky before, they were enfeebled now. Hitler used his emergency powers to ban Communist Party meetings, and called another parliamentary election for March. His Brownshirts stepped up their thuggish activities in the streets.

At Kiel University the Nazis staged a strike against the rector, and Brownshirts from the town joined in the demonstrations on the campus. Fuchs deliberately showed himself before them. He was taking a risk; the Brownshirts had killed political opponents. As it was, they beat him up and threw him in the river.

At home, the members of the Fuchs family decided that they would not talk politics among themselves. Life was becoming dangerous, and they did not want to know too much about one another's activities or contacts, because they could not know how they would respond to interrogation. This inhibition became ingrained, so that fifteen years later, in a very different world, when Emil Fuchs visited his son in England, where he was a scientist holding a senior position, he found that somehow they still shied away from talking about politics.

On the night of 27 February, a mentally unbalanced Dutch tramp with unknown accomplices set fire to the Reichstag, the parliamentary building in Berlin, and what was left of democracy in Germany was consumed in its flames. Even while the building was still blazing, the Nazis blamed the fire on the Communists, and started a reign of terror against opposition parties, arresting 4,000 Communists in the next twenty-four hours. (Evidence was given at the Nuremberg war crimes trials that the Nazis themselves started the Reichstag fire, using the Dutch tramp as a tool.)

Fuchs caught an early train to Berlin the following day, to attend a meeting of student Communists, and read about the fire in a newspaper on the train. He realized the significance right away: the Communists and Social Democrats had both warned that the Nazis might stage a stunt in order to have an excuse to curtail the democratic process in the coming election. He took off the hammer and sickle badge that he was wearing in his lapel and put it in his pocket; from now on, one could not be a Communist openly in Germany.

The meeting in Berlin was held in secret. Fuchs's superiors in the party praised him for his work, and told him he should go abroad and complete his studies, because one day a new, post-Hitler Germany would need qualified people.

He did not return to Kiel after the meeting. He could not go abroad immediately, so he hid in the apartment of a young woman party member. It was a terrible time for him. The Nazis' terror tactics had ensured their victory in the March election, and Germany was being transformed into a Nazi dictatorship. The bully boys who had beaten him up on the streets of Kiel were now the Government.

His fellow Communists and other anti-Nazis were being arrested, beaten, tortured and murdered, and this must have included friends of his.

He was distressed by how little opposition there was. He wrote later, in his confession: 'Not a single party voted against the extraordinary powers which were given to Hitler by the new Reichstag[ii] and in the universities there was hardly anybody who stood up for those who were dismissed either on political or racial grounds, and afterwards you found that people whom you normally would have respected because of their decency had no force in themselves to stand up for their own ideals or moral standards.' His evident disillusionment must have strengthened his conviction that liberal principles were not strong enough to withstand the force of Nazism; that only the Communist Party could fight it effectively, and tight discipline was necessary in the struggle.

One of those dismissed from his post on political grounds was Emil Fuchs. The leaders of the Lutheran Church accepted the Nazi regime, and in many cases made common cause with it (Nazi publications quoted Martin Luther's anti-Jewish tirades), but a small minority of the clergy dissented.

Emil Fuchs was distancing himself from the Lutheran Church on religious as well as social questions. He now doubted the doctrine of the Trinity and the divinity of Jesus, and sought a more direct link between Man and God which did not go by way of miracles and a Messiah. He had been interested for a long time in the Society of Friends, and had many contacts among them. In 1933 he joined the Society, and after this conducted Quaker services.

Klaus Fuchs was in Berlin for five months, in hiding. Then, in August, he went to Paris, to attend an anti-fascist conference under the chairmanship of the French writer Henri Barbusse. The party told him to go; he said later that he was 'sent by the party'. He had very few belongings and very little money, and when he crossed the border, he knew he could not go back.

He was only twenty-one. It must have taken strong nerves, and all the self-assurance his father had noted, to keep his head. He was exiled from his country. All the things that made up the structure of his life — family, friends, career, political activities — had vanished, and he was alone and penniless.

Outside Germany, many people felt revulsion against what was happening there. There was a fund of goodwill and sympathy towards the victims, and this came to Fuchs's rescue. A cousin of his was engaged to a girl who was working as an *au pair* with a wealthy English couple, Ronald and Jessie Gunn, in the village of Clapton in Somerset. Fuchs wrote to her from Paris, telling her of his circumstances. She showed the letter to the Gunns and, generously, they wrote to Fuchs immediately, inviting him to stay with them. Fuchs always said later that the Gunns were Quakers and that he had contacted them through his father's Quaker friends. In fact, there is no record of their having belonged to any Quaker organization; they were Communist sympathizers. It seems that in linking them to the Quakers, Fuchs was trying to protect them from any difficulty that could have arisen from their acting out of political sympathy.

He arrived by Channel steamer at Dover on 24 September 1933, one of the first of a wave of refugees from Nazism who would land on British shores, carrying his few belongings in a bundle; thin, pale and hungry. Because he was going to a village near Bristol, he told the immigration officer that he was planning to study physics at Bristol University; but this was no more than a vague hope, and an answer to give to an official question.

***

Fuchs went to the Bristol area only because of the fortuity of the Gunns' invitation, but had he chosen his location he could hardly have chosen better. Bristol University was not one of the country's biggest, but it had a large and well-equipped physics department that was the equal of any in Britain outside Oxford and Cambridge, thanks to a generous endowment from the Wills family, heirs to the Imperial Tobacco Company. Furthermore, the newly appointed head of the physics department, Professor Nevill Mott, at twenty-eight the youngest full professor in the country, had studied at Göttingen University, spoke fluent German, and also had strong left-wing sympathies. And furthermore, Mrs Jessie Gunn was a member of the Wills family, so the Gunns were in a position to introduce their young house guest to Professor Mott, which they did. They asked him whether he could find a place for Fuchs in his department.

Mott took him on as a research assistant. He was soon glad that he had done so. He found Fuchs very talented and capable although not, perhaps, gifted with the kind of profound intelligence that produces great new discoveries about the nature of things. He was also persistent; if he was given a problem, he would plug away until he had solved it. Mott had a grand scheme to apply quantum mechanics, the mathematics of the shadowy sub-atomic world, to solids, and use this to explain certain properties of the materials. Several of his research assistants worked on aspects of this.

Fuchs was now a changed personality. He was in a strange country, cut off from all his social ties, where he could not even speak or understand the language with any more than a schoolboy's half-forgotten competence. Psychologically as well as legally, he was an alien. He developed caution, the caution of the exile, who does not know how his behaviour or his opinions will be received by the strangers about him. He became reserved, withdrawn, even cold. The political enthusiast who had addressed meetings and argued passionately now spoke very little, and kept his thoughts and feelings to himself. This was the Klaus Fuchs that the world knew from now on.

Always self-contained, as his father had noted, he learned now to do without ties to other people, and withdrew into himself. The self-reliance which had been observed in him when he was a teenager was now vital to him. He relied for assurance only on his own intellectual appreciation of the world. He was a Communist, but he had learned that this was a dangerous thing to be, so he kept it to himself. Perhaps he discussed his political views with the Gunns, who had taken him into their home as a Communist refugee and had friends among German Communists, but he did not discuss them with anyone at the university.

He studied politics, but in the privacy of his room, and he worked out his conclusions in his own mind. Previously, he had thought of Communism primarily in the context of Germany's political situation. Now he looked at it in a worldwide framework. He studied the principles of Marxism, and the Marxist view of the historical process. Like many scientists of the time, he was attracted by Marx's teaching that Man need no longer be at the mercy of historical forces but could now understand and control them, as he was coming to control the forces of nature. Politics was now a part of his private life rather than his public life. It was a matter of deciding what to think rather than what to do.

He did engage briefly in one overt quasi-political activity in Bristol: he did some work for a committee set up to help Spanish Republican refugees in the Spanish Civil War. Most British people may have regarded this as simply an anti-fascist humanitarian group, but so far as he was concerned it was a Communist organization and this was why he helped it.

His physics also was a cerebral activity. It was not experimental or applied, but theoretical physics: the problems were worked out in his own mind. In quantum mechanics in particular, one is working with mathematical terms that do not represent objects at all in the sense that the things in the world about us that we can see and feel are objects. The quantum world is one of paradoxes, of incompatibles, yet when the right mathematics are applied to it, it works. Some physicists are bothered by the philosophical implications of this, and the nature of the reality with which they are dealing, but Fuchs was not of this cast of mind.

He worked on the application of quantum mechanics to explain electrical resistance in the thin films of certain metals. For a while, he worked on this in collaboration with Bernard Lovell, then another young research assistant, later to be Sir Bernard Lovell and one of the founders of the new science of radio-astronomy. Lovell was a robust, cheery young man, and he did not take to his pale, weedy-looking collaborator; he found him too reticent, too bottled-up, for his taste. 'He seems like a chap who's never breathed any fresh air,' he told others. And indeed he did seem rather anaemic-looking: pale-complexioned, with spindly arms and legs and a narrow chest, bespectacled, he was the image of the awkward, unsociable, bookish young scholar.

Bristol University consists of a number of Victorian buildings around the town, which weaves in and out of the fingers of water that contain or used to contain the docks, but the physics building that was built with the Wills family money was newer. The research assistants were mostly young, and keen, and convivial with graduates in other departments. Young men in blazers and pullovers, borrowing money from one another at the end of the month, they would often go to a pub in an evening, or pile into an old car to go somewhere for the weekend. At first someone or other would often ask Fuchs to join them on an outing, but he never accepted and did not encourage such invitations.

Mott was only a little older than the young men working under him, and he was on personal terms with all of them, but he knew almost nothing about Fuchs's background or family. He used to go on long walks in the Mendip Hills with some of his students on Sundays, and Fuchs went along on a few of these, but he walked in silence. His contemporaries at Bristol remember him as an industrious, very talented, very serious young man who talked very little and hardly ever smiled.

Although Fuchs held back from political discussions, Mott persuaded him to come along with him to a few meetings of the Society for Cultural Relations with the Soviet Union. Some of these meetings were devoted to the Moscow treason trials then in progress, at which stalwart leaders of the 1917 Revolution were reduced to puppets, confessing abjectly to preposterous charges that they were Trotskyite agents planning sabotage and assassination at the behest of Western imperialists and Nazi Germany. Most of those attending the meeting wanted to believe that the trials were honest, or at least that there was some honest purpose behind them. Sometimes, in order to achieve a better understanding of what went on in the courtroom, they would act out episodes from the trials.

Fuchs joined in one of these enactments, taking the part of the prosecutor, Andrei Vyshinsky. Mott was surprised to see a new Fuchs: no longer quiet and subdued, he hurled Vyshinsky's denunciations about fiercely. For a few moments, and wearing another's identity, he could reveal his deeply held beliefs.

If he had expressed them more directly, they would have been received sympathetically, all the more so as he had suffered for them at Nazi hands. Many British intellectuals at the time felt goodwill towards Communism, and towards the Soviet Union as a nation that, whatever its faults, was struggling to build a better kind of society, for the Revolution was only twenty years old, in the face of hostility in the capitalist world. Communism was seen widely not as an alternative to democracy but as a new and perhaps richer version of it. Philosophically, it shares the same values as liberal democracy.[iii] Stephen Spender's now-forgotten book about Communism, published in 1937, was called *Forward from Liberalism.* In contrast to the Western democracies — unjust, class-ridden, economically stagnant, half-hearted in their opposition to fascism abroad, particularly in Spain — Russia seemed to be the future that worked, and deserved to work.

The Spanish Civil War dominated political conversation from 1936 onwards, just as the Vietnam War dominated political conversation in the 1960s, and it aroused emotions that were just as strong. The Soviet Union was the only major power to send help to the Spanish Republican side, and Communist Parties around the world supported its cause vigorously.

There was nothing in Fuchs's intellectual environment at this time to challenge the views he held privately; rather, it supported them. This was important in his development.

He did not break entirely with his past. For one thing, he exchanged letters with his father, right up until the outbreak of war. These letters were guarded, but through them, and later through letters from his brother and sister when these had left Germany, he kept in touch with what was happening to his family, although he did not talk about it to anyone in Bristol.

His father Emil was arrested in 1933 for speaking out against the Nazi regime. He was held in prison for a month, and then released on bail, which was put up by a Quaker friend. His trial was delayed for two years. When it came, he appeared before a People's Court, and was unrepentant in his views. However, the regime did not want to offend religious groups any more than necessary, particularly those with strong international connections — a British Quaker was present at his trial. He was sentenced to one month's imprisonment and, as he had already spent a month in prison, he was released immediately.

Gerhardt, the elder son, went to Switzerland and entered a sanatorium where he was treated for tuberculosis. Fuchs went to see him there, his one trip abroad during these years.

His sister Elizabeth had a friend who was also a Communist, Gustav Kittowsky. In 1935 they started a car hire business, and Emil moved to Berlin and joined them in this venture. Elizabeth and Kittowsky married and had a baby son, whom they called Klaus. Kittowsky used to drive abroad, and he used these trips to smuggle Communists out of the country. In 1938 he was caught and sentenced to six years' imprisonment, in a jail in Brandenburg, a Berlin suburb. Elizabeth and Emil used to visit him there, taking little Klaus along.

Kittowsky escaped from prison. He made an arrangement to meet Elizabeth in secret, but did not keep the rendezvous. Then he sent a postcard from Prague. Elizabeth went to live with her father, along with her child. When the Germans occupied Czechoslovakia, in March 1939, she became frantic with worry about Kittowsky's fate (in fact, he survived the war). In August of that year, Emil went to a Quaker conference in Bad Pyrmont, a journey of several hours by train, and he took Elizabeth with him. She seemed so depressed that he became worried, and decided to take her to a doctor when they got back to Berlin. But on the journey back, when he left their compartment for a few moments, she threw herself out. Other passengers pulled the emergency cord, but she was found dead beside the track. He was left with little Klaus, whom he raised by himself.

Fuchs's younger sister, Kristel, had been at a teacher-training college when the Nazis came to power. She went to Switzerland and worked at several jobs there, then went back to Germany and got her teacher's diploma. In 1936 she emigrated to America, and went to Swarthmore College for a time. She travelled by way of England, and had a brief reunion with her brother.

As well as keeping in touch with his family, Fuchs also made contact, after some time, with the German Communist Party, in the person of Jurgen Kuczynski, whom he had probably met in Berlin. Kuczynski was a German Communist of Polish parentage, a few years older than Fuchs, who came to Britain in 1936 and organized German Communist refugees in a number of 'free German' societies. Fuchs did not join any of these. He let Kuczynski know that he was in Britain; he registered with him, so to speak, and thus with the Party. He said later that he may have given him a biography of himself; he could not remember.

Although Fuchs probably did not know this, Kuczynski was an agent of the GRU, the overseas intelligence branch of the Soviet Army. He had been recruited while on a visit to Moscow. He was thus a member of that international army of volunteers who had enlisted in the 1920s and 1930s to serve in secret the cause of world revolution. His sister Ruth was another. They joined at a time when it was much easier than it is now to believe in this revolution, and to believe that it was for the betterment of humanity, and to believe also that it was best advanced by serving the interests of the Soviet state. Some, like Kuczynski, were openly Communist Party members, while serving also as Soviet intelligence agents. Others had no overt connection with Communism, and served either as spies or as agents of influence. This invisible army became visible only occasionally, with an arrest, such as that of the Belgian who inveigled his way into Trotsky's entourage in Mexico and stabbed him to death, or of the Krogers, the American couple living in London who were part of a spy ring, or an occasional defection, such as that of the Briton Alexander Foote, who worked with both Kuczynski and his sister in Switzerland.

Fuchs also registered his presence with the German Consulate in Bristol. In 1934 he wrote to the Consulate asking for the renewal of his passport. The Consul refused, and said he could have only a temporary travel document permitting him to return to Germany. The Consulate also told the British police that Fuchs was a Communist. In 1936 Fuchs received a notice from the Consulate ordering him to report for military service, which was now compulsory in Germany, and he ignored it.

After Fuchs had been with the Gunns for a year, they moved to a large house in Bristol and he moved with them, remaining their house guest. Two years later he took a room in a boarding-house, while remaining on good terms with them.

He was at Bristol University for four years, and earned a PhD there. At the end of that time he spoke good English, although with a strong German accent which he was never to lose. He had established himself in a career. He met there people he was to meet again later: Herbert Skinner, then a lecturer, who was to become a close friend at Harwell, and Hans Bethe, a young visiting scholar from Germany who already had a high reputation and who was to be his boss on the atom bomb project at Los Alamos. A paper of his, 'A Quantum Mechanical Calculation of the Elastic Constance of Monovalent Metals', was published in the *Proceedings of the Royal Society* in February 1936.

By this time, Mott had six German refugees working in his department, and he knew he could get tenure for only three. He decided that Fuchs should be one of the ones to go, partly because he had completed his research project.

The normal next step would be a teaching post, but Mott felt that Fuchs was too uncommunicative to be a good teacher. So he wrote to Max Born, one of the greatest German physicists of the 1930s diaspora, whom he had known at Göttingen and who was now at Edinburgh University, recommending Fuchs for a research post. Born accepted him and, after a brief farewell to Bristol, the Gunns and Mott, Fuchs moved north to the Scottish capital.

***

Born took to Fuchs; he found him, as he recalled later, 'a very nice, quiet fellow with sad eyes'. They became friends, although Fuchs maintained his reserve and Born was aware that he knew nothing of Fuchs's private thoughts. He also found him gifted as a mathematical physicist, and enlisted him in projects in several different areas of theoretical physics. They published two papers together in the *Proceedings of the Royal Society,* 'The Statistical Mechanics of Condensing Systems' and 'On Fluctuations in Electromagnetic Radiation'; Fuchs proudly sent these to his father in Germany. Fuchs and Born also published another paper in an academic journal, 'The Equation of State in a Dense Gas'. Fuchs's professional status was enhanced by the coupling of his name with Born's in these papers. He also earned a further degree at Edinburgh University, that of Doctor of Science.

He was a little less of a loner than he had been at Bristol. He came to be on friendly terms with two others in the physics department, and saw quite a lot of them: Hans Kellerman, another young German refugee who had an open, easy-going manner that was quite different to Fuchs's own, and an idiosyncratic, highly strung young American, Edward Corson. Fuchs exchanged letters with the Gunns, and Ronald Gunn wrote him a long letter about his views on free will and determinism.

He kept the letters that the Gunns wrote to him. He kept most of the personal letters that anyone wrote to him. In 1950 he had some 250 letters he had received over the years. It was as if, with his limited human contact, he wanted these tangible signs of the contact that he did have.

The years at Bristol and Edinburgh were Fuchs's twenties, a decade for most people in which they develop an adult personality, acquire a direction, embark on a career, learn to relate to other people, particularly to the opposite sex, and acquire lasting friendships. At the end of the decade Fuchs was well established in a career, but he was only beginning to find a way to relate to other people, or to rediscover a way, after the break in his life when he left Germany. He had no close relationships with women and, in personality terms, his principal achievement was learning to live without other people rather than learning to live with them. He had established a moat between his own emotional life and those of others, and he was building his life on one side of it.

In Edinburgh, he also carried out one more service for the German Communist Party. Kuczynski organized the sending of Communist leaflets to Germany. Fuchs played a part in this, posting some of the leaflets.

In August 1939, the Soviet Union signed a non-aggression pact with Nazi Germany. This was a shock to friends of the Soviet Union. Some could not stomach it. Many Communists found the news shattering but most, after discussing it among themselves, concluded that it was a justifiable tactical manoeuvre, because, with Britain and France refusing to join Russia in a united front against Germany, Russia had to buy time. Fuchs also was shocked, more so than most because he had joined the Communist Party precisely to fight against Nazism. He thrashed this over in his own mind, and worried about it without the give-and-take of discussion with other people. He also concluded eventually that it was justified.

Three months later Russia took another move that affronted many of its friends: it invaded Finland, in order to seize the strategically important area of Karelia. This time, Fuchs allowed himself the luxury of defending Russia openly, in a discussion with Born, arguing that the invasion was a defensive measure in preparation for the war which Russia expected.

Fuchs applied for British citizenship in August 1939. But the following month war broke out, and as a German he became an enemy alien, so his application was set aside. A system of classification of enemy aliens was set up, dividing them into A, B and C categories. C meant that they were not likely to be a security risk and were not to be subject to any restrictions; eighty per cent of the 50,000 Germans in Britain, most of them Jewish refugees, were put into this category. Everyone had to appear before a tribunal: when Fuchs was summoned, Born wrote to the tribunal assuring them that Fuchs had been a member of the Social Democratic Party in Germany between 1930 and 1932, and Fuchs himself told them that he was a sincere anti-Nazi. He was given a C classification.

This was the period of the so-called phoney war, in which there was very little fighting. Some newspapers speculated that Germany would collapse economically and the war would be over soon. Then, suddenly, everything changed. In May and June 1940 the German armies overran Belgium, Holland and France with bewildering speed, and positioned themselves on the shores of the English Channel. Britain was faced with invasion, by an enemy that had shown itself to be terrifyingly efficient at fighting a war. In the atmosphere of alarm, wild rumours went around of spies and saboteurs; exaggerated accounts were published of the activities of fifth columnists on the Continent and their contribution to the German victory. In particular, there were stories from Holland of Germans who had posed as refugees from Nazism but had turned out to be secret agents helping the advancing German armies. The War Office demanded that all enemy aliens be interned immediately as a precautionary measure.

One morning in late June, a policeman appeared at Fuchs's door and told him to pack some things and come to the police station. Within hours he was on his way, along with thousands of others, to a hastily organized internment camp on the Isle of

Man. He did not even have a chance to let Born know he was not coming in to work. Kellerman was picked up on the same day.

Fuchs's sojourn on the Isle of Man was brief, for measures were already being taken to transport enemy aliens further away from the war zone, to places where they could do no harm, in Canada and Australia. On 3 July Fuchs boarded the liner *Ettrick* in Liverpool, bound for Quebec. His fellow passengers were some 1,300 other internees from the Isle of Man, 750 German prisoners of war and 400 Italian prisoners of war. Another liner, the *Arandora Star,* had sailed three days earlier flying a swastika below the Red Ensign to let the Germans know she was carrying prisoners of war, but she was torpedoed and sunk twenty-four hours after leaving port. The *Ettrick* set sail also with a swastika flag and Red Ensign, but then the news of the *Arandora Star's* fate was received and it was realized that this provided no protection, so the *Ettrick* returned to Liverpool, and sailed the following day in a convoy, with a destroyer escort.

The crossing was uncomfortable and the arrival unpropitious. As often happened in wartime, the prisoners of war were treated better than the internees, because the prisoners of war were under the protection of the Geneva Convention and their treatment was governed by its rules, whereas the Government was answerable to no one and no set rules in its treatment of internees. The internees were kept in the hold and had to stay below decks for the whole journey. The sea was rough and many people were sick, and there was also an outbreak of diarrhoea. Most of them recall the crossing as a nightmare.

The arrival was not a happy one. The authorities in Quebec were not at first aware that there were anti-Nazi refugees on board, and thought that they were receiving dangerous Nazis that the British wanted out of the way. The *Ettrick* was met by armed soldiers who lined up the passengers at bayonet point, searched them thoroughly and kept them under close guard.

Some also pilfered their belongings. (A year later the Canadian and British Governments jointly paid compensation to those who were robbed.) Some of the more sophisticated among the Canadian soldiers were puzzled by the presence of three rabbis among these supposed Nazis.

They were all sent to a camp at Sherbrooke, on the Plains of Abraham, outside Quebec City, with a magnificent panoramic view of the St Lawrence River and the hills beyond. It was a Canadian Army camp which was adapted for internment purposes by ringing it with barbed wire and a wire fence.

The occupants were certainly treated as prisoners, and occasionally bullied by guards. Restrictions were placed upon them — on the amount of mail they could send and receive, for instance — and one mentally unbalanced young man who had been in a concentration camp was shot dead trying to escape, in a tragic accident that was hushed up at the time. Yet in many ways life was not all that unpleasant, and most of the internees were aware that their relatives and friends in their homeland were suffering very much worse. They were eating considerably better than they had in Britain, where wartime rationing was in force, and they were spared the dangers and discomfort of air raids on British cities. The internees were for the most part a highly educated and motivated group. They organized camp activities, musical entertainments and a camp university. They also organized high school classes for some young people who had been coming up for their matriculation exams when they were pulled out of school.

Intellectual life flourished. One inmate was elected a fellow of Trinity College, Cambridge while he was in the camp, and another received his PhD there. (This is not the place to go into details but, judging from the subsequent achievements of Camp Sherbrooke alumni in many fields, this must have been the most remarkable assemblage of intellect ever to have been gathered in one prison. Just for instance, when the steady state theory of the nature of the universe was propounded by three astronomers and physicists, Thomas Gold, Sir Herman Bondi and Fred Hoyle, it turned out that two of them had been Sherbrooke internees: Gold, who is now Director of the Centre for Space Research at Cornell University, and Bondi, who some years after having been deported from Britain as a potentially dangerous alien, became Chief Scientist at the Ministry of Defence.)

The camp authorities appointed as the prisoners' spokesman Prince Friedrich of Prussia, Count Lingen, a grandson of the Kaiser, an anti-Nazi German who had been studying farming methods in England when war broke out. The other internees regarded their prince as something of a curiosity, but he was always decent and courteous in his behaviour and was well liked. It was said that he gained some influence over the camp commandant (who read outgoing mail) by writing letters to the wife of the Governor-General of Canada, Princess Alice, Countess of Athlone, addressing her as 'Dear Aunt Alice'. Certainly his Aunt Alice sent him a football, at his request, for the inmates to use.

Fuchs was unusual among the internees, although not unique, in that he was not Jewish. He said later that he resented being interned along with Nazis, of whom there were a number in the camp, but in general he showed little bitterness and understood the anxieties of the British Government of the time.

Being among Germans again, he reverted to his Communist past and dropped his concealment of his Communist beliefs. He used to attend the regular weekly discussion meeting of a group of Communists and fellow travellers which was formed in the camp, although he rarely spoke at these meetings. The leader of the group was Hans Kahle, a German Communist who had commanded the Eleventh International Brigade in the Spanish Civil War. Kahle was one of the celebrities of the camp, widely liked and admired by Communists and non-Communists alike. He had been a friend of Ernest Hemingway in Spain, and Hemingway sent him an inscribed copy of his Spanish Civil War novel, *For Whom the Bell Tolls,* while he was in the camp.

Fuchs was called on by the organizers of the camp university to give lectures in physics, which he did, mostly to scientists in other fields. His lectures were lucid and well attended. Apart from this he remained a loner, spoke little and made few friends. However, he was liked, and an affectionate diminutive was added to his name — he was called 'Fuchslein', which means 'little fox'. When fellow internees recalled him long afterwards, when he was arrested as a spy, one called him an 'oddball', another 'aloof' and another said simply that he was 'reserved'. One, Martin Wallich, who was a BBC radio producer by then, expressed surprise that the authorities had not known he was a Communist, since his membership in Kahle's group at the camp was no secret.

Apart from his participation in this group, there was one other link between Fuchs and the world of professional Communists, which was none of his doing. He was corresponding with his sister Kristel, who had emigrated to America. She was now married and living in Cambridge, Massachusetts. She talked about Fuchs to people she knew, and one of these, Wendell Furry, told her he had a brother-in-law in Canada, and would ask him to contact Fuchs. This brother-in-law was Israel Halperin, a mathematics professor at Queen's University, in Kingston, Ontario. Halperin sent Fuchs some magazines, although the two never met. When the Soviet spy ring in Canada was broken in 1946 Halperin, a member of the Canadian Communist Party, was found to be acquainted with several of those convicted. Police searched his home and found an address book containing Fuchs's name.

Kristel wrote to Fuchs saying: 'I hope to see you now that you are in the Western hemisphere.' But Born in Edinburgh was pressing for his release, as others pressed for the release of other internees. Six months after the camp was established the first group of 287 inmates were freed and sent back to England, and Fuchs was among them. (So were Count Lingen and Kahle.) They sailed from Halifax on Christmas Day, on the Belgian ship *Thysville*. Fuchs was able to resume his work at Edinburgh University.

***

In the spring of 1941 Fuchs received a letter from the Professor of Mathematical Physics at Birmingham University, Rudolf Peierls, another German refugee a few years his senior who had recently become a British citizen. Fuchs knew Peierls slightly, having met him when he visited Bristol University, and again at Edinburgh. It was a letter that was to change his life; what Peierls was doing in Birmingham was to change all our lives. To appreciate the significance of this letter, it is necessary to recall some of the background of events.

By the early 1930s physicists had worked out the internal structure of the atom: a nucleus of protons and neutrons, with electrons whirling around it in orbits. They began to manipulate these particles, using their electrical properties. They built machines that could project them, through electrical attraction or repulsion.

Physicists do not discover the behaviour of these particles by observing them, in the way that biologists observe minute living cells. No one has ever seen an atom, let alone one of its constituent particles, and no one ever will. They do it by analysing the effects of the motions of these particles, on the basis of what they presume to be the reality of the sub-atomic world. They produce these effects by experiments, a process often requiring extraordinary ingenuity and imagination.

In the 1930s these experiments were going on in several places in Europe and America. The scientists carrying them out had several characteristics in common. Most of them were young for people who were advancing the frontiers of knowledge so dramatically, many in their twenties and early thirties. Most of them knew each other: they had passed through the same universities and attended the same international conferences. Sharing the same excitement about new discoveries that few others could comprehend, many of them became close friends, and would remain so for the rest of their lives. Also, a large proportion of them were Jewish, products of a humanistic, central European cultural background that fostered both intellectual interests and humane social concerns, and these were to leave the Continent with the rise of Nazism, mostly for Britain and America.

The analysis of one particular experiment provided a puzzle. Enrico Fermi in Rome had been bombarding minute quantities of elements with neutrons. This would knock away one or two particles to produce a slightly different substance. But when he and then Irene Curie in Paris did this with the heaviest element, uranium, two German chemists, Otto Hahn and Fritz Strassman, analysed the results and, in 1938, they found traces of barium apparently resulting from it. Now barium is not a slightly different kind of substance from uranium, but a very different kind. It weighs only about half as much; its atom has 137 particles, while a uranium atom has 238. A neutron cannot knock 101 particles out of an atom. Hahn and Strassman published their findings, and left it to others to provide an explanation.

Hahn also wrote about his findings to a former colleague of his, Lise Meitner, an Austrian and one of the few women to distinguish herself in the field of physics. She had to leave Germany because she was Jewish, and was now at the Nobel Institute in Stockholm. Hahn's letter arrived at Christmastime 1938, when Dr Meitner was entertaining her nephew, Otto Frisch. He was also a physicist, and had worked in Germany until the advent of Hitler, and was now at the Niels Bohr Institute in Copenhagen.

The two pondered Hahn's letter together during a long walk through the snow-covered countryside, and then Lise Meitner had an idea. She suggested that a uranium atom might be unstable in such a way that if a neutron were injected, it would split up into two roughly equal parts. They sat down on a log and tested the idea on the spot by working out the mathematics, and it seemed to come out right. Then Frisch designed and carried out an experiment to test the theory, and this seemed to confirm it.

They collaborated on a paper setting out this idea, and finished it in a series of telephone conversations when Frisch was back in Copenhagen. At one point Frisch asked an American biologist at the Bohr Institute what biologists call it when a cell divides spontaneously, and he said the word was 'fission'. So Frisch described the splitting of the uranium atom as 'atomic fission', and he used this term in the paper, which was published in the British scientific journal *Nature* in February 1939.

Several physicists immediately spotted a possibility that was not mentioned in this paper. A uranium atom contains a lot of neutrons, and some of these would go flying off when the atom is split and split other uranium atoms in turn, in a chain reaction. When particles leave an atom, energy is released. The cumulative effect of a chain reaction could be a release of energy so rapid, and so great, that it would constitute a very powerful explosion.

Until this moment, atomic physics had been the most abstract of sciences, far removed from any practical application. Now, suddenly, it seemed that there might after all be a practical application. The US Government set up an Advisory Committee on Uranium to look into the possibility of a uranium bomb, and individual scientists explored the idea and carried out experiments.

In the summer of 1939 Otto Frisch was offered a teaching post at Birmingham University. He accepted, partly in order to place some more distance between himself and the Nazi regime, and he arrived in England just a few days before the outbreak of war. Peierls, an old friend and fellow adventurer on the frontiers of physics, was already at Birmingham. Frisch, a bachelor, stayed for a while in an uncomfortable boarding-house; then, as Peierls and his wife Eugenia had rented a large, three-storey house near the university, they invited him to move in with them, and he lived there for several months.

Frisch, having set off speculation about the possibility of a bomb that worked by uranium fission, examined the problem further. It was becoming clear that only one kind of uranium atom, which made up less than one per cent of the total, actually split. He concluded that this would make a fission bomb — or a super-bomb, as it was coming to be called — impossible. He was asked to write a contribution on advances in this area for the *Annual Report of the Chemical Society,* and he reported this in his paper. Peierls examined the possibility and came to the same conclusion. This was now the prevailing view in Britain and America, and the considered opinion of the US Government's Uranium Committee: that a super-bomb was either impossible or else so very distant that there was no point in devoting resources to the prospect at present.

However, Frisch and Peierls found that their minds were still working on the subject, and would not stop. They talked about it in the evenings in the Peierls' living-room.

The atom that fissions is an isotope of uranium called uranium 235. An isotope is a variant of an atom that is chemically indistinguishable, but has slightly more or slightly fewer neutrons. This particular isotope has three fewer neutrons — 235 particles altogether instead of 238; hence the number, u-235. What, Frisch asked, if you could isolate a quantity of uranium 235? Could it be done? He and Peierls worked out the mathematics of a u-235 chain reaction, and found to their surprise that the amount needed to create an explosion was not a few tons, as they had thought, but a few pounds. And they decided that it would be possible to isolate this amount of uranium 235. Frisch wrote later: 'At that point, we stared at each other, and realized that an atomic bomb might after all be possible.'

They set out their reasoning and their calculations in a memorandum. The bomb would be made with uranium 235, and they made a suggestion as to how this could be separated from ordinary uranium. They calculated the critical size, the size of the mass of u-235 which would explode (underestimating it). They described the mechanism for exploding the bomb: two pieces of u-235 which together added up to the critical mass would be brought together with great speed. They described its effects, including radiation. Their key sentence was: 'We have... come to the conclusion that a moderate amount of u-235 would indeed constitute an extremely efficient explosive.' This memorandum is the first suggestion of how an atomic bomb could be built, and it is one of the historic documents of the twentieth century.

They took it to Mark Oliphant, a senior physicist at the university who was working on radar and was therefore in touch with the defence authorities. He fed it into the governmental machine. The result was the setting up of a committee, christened the Maud Committee, in April 1940 to explore the possibility of producing either power or explosives from nuclear fission. It came under the Ministry of Aircraft Production. Work was farmed out to scientists at Oxford, Cambridge and Liverpool Universities. Peierls and Frisch continued their work at Birmingham, but in the summer of 1940 Frisch moved to Liverpool, to work under James Chadwick, using Britain's only cyclotron. Many of the scientists involved in this work were refugees from the Continent, simply because most British-born physicists were already working in military technology, mostly to do with radar.

A spur to everyone's efforts in this area was the fear that German physicists might be working along the same lines, and might be first with a super-bomb. Many leading nuclear physicists were German, and some of them were still in Germany. The German victories of 1940, which left Britain alone and vulnerable, and the German air attacks which were to be a prelude to invasion, gave an even greater sense of urgency to every kind of war work. If the prospect of Nazi occupation was still unimaginable to most British people, it was all too real to people who had come from countries where the Nazis now ruled, and, if they were Jewish, it was particularly threatening.

The Peierls took the painful step of sending their young son and daughter to Canada for safety, taking advantage of a scheme devised for university faculty families. Peierls had been struck particularly by the sight of Home Guard units drilling with shotguns, and he envisioned them confronting Panzer divisions. (He was willing to face the danger himself. Early in 1939 his friend Hans Bethe had written from America suggesting that he might like to come and work there. He wrote back saying that it looked as if the Chamberlain Government would continue its appeasement policy indefinitely, and this would mean that democracy in Europe was beaten, in which case he would like to come to America; if, however, Britain resisted and there was a war, he would remain and play what part he could.) Peierls became an auxiliary fireman as well as a physicist, spending nights fighting fires started by German bombs, for Birmingham, as a major industrial centre, was a target for the Luftwaffe when the air raids on Britain started. Mrs Peierls became an auxiliary nurse at a local hospital; later she switched jobs and became a fitter in a GEC plant making aircraft components.

In early 1941 Peierls decided that he needed an assistant. He remembered his brief meetings with Klaus Fuchs, and remembered also some of Fuchs's papers that he had read and discussed with him. These papers showed mathematical skill, and also flexibility, and this was a quality he thought would be needed on this project, since they were going into unexplored territory and there was no way of knowing what problems they would encounter. Fuchs had not done any work on atomic fission but that was not important; it was talent, not expertise, that was wanted.

Peierls asked the Ministry of Aircraft Production whether he might recruit Fuchs. The Ministry asked MI5, the domestic counter-intelligence service, whether anything untoward was known about Fuchs. MI5 had two items about him in their files. One was the 1934 report from the German consul in Bristol that he was a Communist, but this was from a tainted source. The other was more recent: a report from an informant in the German refugee community saying that, he was known to be a Communist. This was not without significance. At this time the Nazi-Soviet Non-Aggression Pact was in operation and the British Communist Party, following the Soviet line, argued for peace with Germany. Communists were suspected of sabotaging the war effort and the party newspaper, the *Daily Worker,* was banned under wartime emergency regulations.

The report on Fuchs may have had some influence, but it was not much. Perhaps because of it, a Ministry official replied to Peierls saying he could hire Fuchs, provided he told him only what he needed to know for the problem he was working on. Peierls wrote back saying that he could not work that way, that if he had an assistant he would have to take him fully into the picture. The Ministry official dropped the condition and told him to go ahead.

Peierls wrote to Fuchs in Edinburgh offering him the job. He gave no indication of what the work was, but told him that it could be important to the war effort. The salary was £275 a year, probably as much as he was earning in Edinburgh; it was to rise to £400 in the next two years.

Fuchs accepted Peierls's offer. He said later that he had no idea what the work involved, but if he had known it would not have made any difference. He wrote a letter of acceptance, and in May 1941 he packed his belongings and took a train south through blacked-out Britain to Birmingham, to join the mainstream of twentieth-century history.

CHAPTER TWO

Housing was short in wartime Birmingham, and the Peierls invited Fuchs to move in with them when he came down from Edinburgh, in their large house in Culthorpe Road, in the Edgbaston district. He accepted, taking the room that Otto Frisch had vacated a few months earlier.

Rudolf and Eugenia Peierls (now Sir Rudolf and Lady Peierls) are a contrasting couple. He is quiet and self-effacing, modest about his achievements, usually willing to yield the floor in a conversation. She is warm, outgoing and exuberant, speaking volubly in a heavy Russian accent that she has never lost, although she left Russia in 1931.

Their courtship had the romance of exotic locations and love overcoming obstacles. They met in Odessa on the Black Sea when he, a twenty-three-year-old German physicist at the University of Zürich, was attending a conference on physics there. She had recently graduated in physics at Leningrad University, and had gone to the conference at her own expense out of interest. They both spoke English, and this was the only language they had in common. They talked together for ten days, and when he went back to Zürich and she to her home in Leningrad, they corresponded, in English. He visited her in Leningrad and proposed, and they were married there. Then he returned to Zürich, and they had to wait six months before the Soviet authorities would allow her to leave and join him.

In 1932 Peierls was in the happy position of being able to divide his time between Fermi's laboratory in Rome and the Rutherford Laboratory at Cambridge University, thanks to a Rockefeller Foundation grant given for this purpose. He was offered an attractive university post in Hamburg, and he accepted. Then Franz von Papen became Chancellor of Germany, and the Peierls foresaw a rapid slide downwards leading to Hitler; they are both Jewish. He changed his mind about the Hamburg post and accepted an offer from Manchester University, joining those central Europeans whose lives were determined by political events.

Fuchs was an easy person to live with. He gave his ration books to the Peierls and ate his meals with them. He used to help with the dishes after supper, and usually spent the rest of the evening in his room, which he always kept tidy. He was then twenty-nine, an excessively quiet, thin man of medium height, wearing glasses, with plain features and a prominent Adam's apple: he had long, strong fingers that could belong to a pianist, that often held a cigarette.

Eugenia Peierls is very gregarious, so that despite their extra war work as fireman and nurse the couple often had people in the house. Fuchs was always present but stayed in the background, and usually spoke only when spoken to. A frequent guest was a Russian emigre who was a specialist in linguistics at the university; they often discussed Russia and Russian literature, but Fuchs rarely joined in these conversations.

Explaining his reticence to others, Mrs Peierls coined a phrase that both she and her husband were to use about Fuchs many times. 'He's a penny-in-the-slot person,' she said. 'Put a question in and you get an answer out. But if you don't put anything in, you don't get anything out.' By now, Fuchs was relaxed enough so that she could tease him about this, and he would grin sheepishly.

Mrs Peierls never felt his silences discomfiting. 'There are some people,' she explained to a friend, 'who don't say much and you feel it's because they're shy, that they want to speak but are afraid to. This makes me uncomfortable. I never feel that with Klaus.'

He told the Peierls about his internment camp in Canada, and said he resented being lumped together with Nazis. He talked a little about university days in Germany, and his activities with the student Socialists. He never said that he was a Communist, although Peierls would not have been deterred from hiring him, and would not have thought less of him, if he had. People talked politics and talked about the war. Fuchs rarely expressed political opinions; he left a vague impression that he was a democratic Socialist and blended in, as he had in Bristol, with the moderate left-wing background.

If he was self-contained emotionally and intellectually, he was dependent in other ways. He had little social competence. Mrs Peierls used to tell him when and how to get his laundry done and when to change his suit, and she used to remind him to send Christmas cards. With her children away, she took naturally to this mothering role. She used to choose most of her husband's clothes, and when she decided that he needed a new suit, she would take him around the shops. Now she did the same for Fuchs.

Meanwhile, the Maud Committee's work was advancing rapidly. In July 1941 Sir George Thomson, the Committee's chairman, wrote a report for the Cabinet's Scientific Advisory Committee saying that on the basis of the work done so far, there seemed a good chance that a uranium fission bomb could be produced before the end of the war. As a result, a full programme to build an atomic bomb was authorized, with the deliberately misleading name Tube Alloys.

Britain and the United States had been exchanging information on scientific work with military potential since the outbreak of war, and this included information on atomic fission. The optimistic report of the Maud Committee was sent to America, where it was seen by the Uranium Committee. Previously, this committee had reported that it was doubtful that an atomic bomb could be produced in time to have any effect on the course of the war. After seeing the Maud Committee's report, they thought again, and a new committee was set up under the National Academy of Sciences. This committee recommended that work begin.

Two American physicists, Harold Urey and G. B. Pegram, were sent to Britain to make their own report. They were given access to all the British work. They visited the centres and saw the scientists involved, including Peierls and Fuchs, and took back with them an enthusiastic account of British progress. President Roosevelt considered both these optimistic reports, and in the first week of December 1941 he gave the go-ahead for a new organization to set about building an atomic bomb. At the end of that week, the Japanese bombed Pearl Harbor, Germany declared war on the United States, and the war became World War II.

Peierls and Fuchs were working on two tasks. One was doing theoretical calculations of nuclear fission reactions, which would show among other things how much uranium 235 would be needed for a bomb. The other was working out how to isolate uranium 235, for it was already becoming clear that this would be a major problem. The separation of isotopes is always difficult, because there is no chemical difference between them. The less difference there is in atomic number, and therefore weight, the more difficult it is to separate them. It is usually easy to distinguish between two objects if one is twice the weight of the other, as deuterium, an isotope of hydrogen, is twice the weight of ordinary hydrogen; it is much more difficult if the difference is only three parts in 238, as is the difference between uranium 235 and 238. It is easier to separate basketballs from tennis balls than basketballs from another kind of basketball that is fractionally heavier.

The separation method suggested in the Frisch-Peierls Memorandum, involving a heat transfer process, proved not to be viable. The favoured method was now a process of diffusion: the uranium would be turned into a gas and passed through membranes, so that more of the heavier atoms would be left behind and the lighter ones passed through. A pilot plant to try out this method was built at Valley, in North Wales, and scientists there got a taste of the horrendous problems involved in the process. The membranes had to be finer than any ever constructed before: the first specifications were for membranes one-thousandth of an inch thick perforated with holes one-ten-thousandth of an inch in diameter. Furthermore the gas, uranium hexafluoride, turned out to be very corrosive. Fuchs visited the plant, and saw the translation of his calculations into physical reality.

Peierls had every reason to be pleased with his choice of assistant. Fuchs was an excellent mathematician, and also he showed just the flexibility that Peierls had hoped for. Confronted with a new problem, he was quick to grasp the essentials. A Tube Alloys directorate was set up with a small office in London, and scientists working on different aspects of the project were required to send in monthly reports on their work. Fuchs always got his reports in on time, unlike many of the others; they were lucid — he wrote English easily by now — and he showed the same ability to pick out essentials.

At about this time, Peierls noticed a certain arrogance in Fuchs's attitude. He always looked up to Peierls; however, when they went over papers they received from America on the work being done there, Peierls was ready to learn from them if there was anything new, but Fuchs's attitude seemed to be, 'Let's see if the Americans are working on the right lines.' Others, over the years, even at Bristol, remarked that although Fuchs was withdrawn, he never seemed unsure of himself. He had confidence in his own reasoning powers.

While the Maud Committee report was being prepared in the summer of 1941, something else of historic importance occurred. On 22 June, Germany attacked the Soviet Union. Instantly, the world situation was transformed. Russia was no longer a partner with Germany in a nonaggression pact, but was fighting for its life against it. Communist parties around the world threw their weight behind the war against Germany. They did so with a will. Communists had accepted that the Nazi-Soviet pact was tactically correct, as Fuchs did, but it left a bad taste in the mouth; Nazism and its values were hateful to them. Now Nazi Germany was the enemy once again and things were in their proper place.

Fuchs knew that the project he was working on was potentially of great military significance. Perhaps he would have acted as he did if Germany had not invaded the Soviet Union, but Russia's plight must have given him added impetus.

He took a momentous step. It was probably less momentous for him than it would be for most people. In his searching eight-page confession, in which he analysed his motives, he devoted just one sentence to it: 'When I learned the purpose of the work, I decided to inform Russia and I established contact through another member of the Communist Party.' (The phrase 'another member' is interesting, for it indicates that he considered himself at that time still a member.)

Most of us have ties that might inhibit us from acting on strict political or even moral logic: ties created by background, environment, and family and other personal loyalties. We obey the law as a matter of habit. Setting out to give information to a foreign power would mean breaking out of the framework of laws and customs in which we live our lives.

But Fuchs had none of these ties, and there was no framework to break through. He had grown up in a German society in which the outlines were fluid, one that did not command the natural loyalty of all its citizens. Although he had applied for British citizenship, he did not seem to consider himself to be a part of British society. The flag of his native land was now the swastika, which he had every reason to hate. His only national commitment was to a Germany that did not yet exist, the post-Nazi Germany for which he had been told to prepare himself when he left Berlin. His only tie of loyalty was the one he had worked out in his own mind, to the abstraction of Communism; and because of this to a country that was, for him, hardly less abstract, the Soviet Union.

On a visit to London in late 1941, he looked up his old acquaintance Jurgen Kuczynski, and told him that he had some information that could be of value to the Soviet Union. Kuczynski said he would find him someone to pass it on to, and asked to see him again. Presumably, as a GRU agent, he contacted his GRU network. He arranged a contact for Fuchs, a man Fuchs would know only as Alexander. This was in fact Simon Davidovitch Kremer, a member of the military attaché's staff at the Soviet Embassy.

Now, for Fuchs, politics would be once again a matter of doing something and not just thinking something. He would be an acting Communist again, and not just a believer.

Helping the cause of Communism meant helping the Soviet Union. To a Marxist, the world is divided horizontally into classes; the vertical division into nations is a superficial one. The crucial division is between the working class and the capitalist class. Events that are described conventionally in terms of the vertical division, as relations between nations, are reinterpreted in terms of the horizontal division, as relations between classes, by a process similar to a mathematical transformation in which a formula represented by a line on a graph is rotated through an angle of 90 degrees. When the Soviet Union was the only Communist country, this meant identifying the interests of the working class all over the world, in the horizontal division, with those of the Soviet Union, in the vertical one.

The Soviet Union was the country in which Communist principles were being put into practice, and from which Communism as a liberating force would spread. The Comintern, the Communist International, had declared: 'Since the Soviet Union is the true fatherland of the proletariat, the strongest pillar of its achievements, and the principal factor in its emancipation throughout the world, this obliges the international proletariat to forward the success of Socialist construction in the Soviet Union, and to defend the country of the proletariat dictatorship by every means.'

Communists were quite open about this. The issue was raised in France in 1949 when the physicist Frederic Joliot-Curie, removed from his post in the French Atomic Energy Commission because he was a Communist, told a meeting of journalists that no honest Frenchman, Communist or otherwise, would deliver national secrets to a foreign power. He was rebuked by the Secretary of the French Communist Party, Jacques Duclos, who said: 'Every progressive has two fatherlands, his own and the Soviet Union.' And the party bureau told a Communist newspaper: 'M Joliot-Curie has committed the error of including the USSR, the fatherland of all workers, in the phrase "any foreign power". A French Communist should have no secrets from the USSR.'

There seemed to be very little gap between Fuchs deciding in his own mind that a course of action was morally right, and acting on the decision. After all, his father's teaching to his children was that they should *do* what they thought was right.

Fuchs typed his reports on the calculations of nuclear fission and uranium diffusion, and made carbon copies, and he took these carbon copies with him when he went to his first meeting with Kremer. This was at a house near Hyde Park, not far from the Soviet Embassy. He gave the papers to Kremer, and they arranged a second meeting. Then Fuchs had a spasm of doubt about whether this man he knew only as Alexander was who he said he was, and whether those papers would really reach the Soviet authorities; so on his next visit to London he went to the Soviet Embassy to find out. Kremer saw him there and reassured him, although he could hardly have been pleased at this breach of security.

Fuchs met Kremer three times during the next six months. Each time he gave him copies of his reports, either typed or handwritten. Kremer gave him some elementary lessons in being a spy, which he did not always accept. He told him to take taxis, and double-back on his route to throw off anyone who might be following. Fuchs remarked prosaically that this would be expensive. Kremer also told him that if he thought he was being followed, he should cross the street and go into an empty building or some other empty place and see if anyone came after. Fuchs suggested they meet in large and busy places, which they did: a station, and a busy shopping street.

In the autumn of 1942, Kremer told Fuchs he was passing him on to another contact, a woman he would know only as Sonja. He would not have to go to London to meet her, but could see her closer to Birmingham. Sonja was, in fact, Ruth Kuczynski, Jurgen's sister, although of course Fuchs did not know this. Like her brother, she was a long-time GRU agent, serving the cause as a devoted volunteer, and had worked in China and Switzerland. A dark-haired, attractive woman, she chose her lovers and then her husband from the ranks of the Soviet Intelligence network. Now she was living in the village of Kidlington, near Oxford, with her British husband, who was shortly to join the Army, and in the course of time three children.[iv] For the GRU it was an advantage that, unlike Kremer, she had no connection with the Soviet Embassy.

For the next eighteen months or so, Fuchs used to meet her regularly in Banbury, a market town some thirty-five miles from Birmingham and ten miles from her home. They did not meet in crowded places but in a country lane, or, on one occasion, at a cafe near the station. Each time he passed over papers he had written.

In the main, he was still operating on the strict Protestant principle that each person is responsible for his own conscience. He handed over only his own work. He would not hand over work by Peierls or anyone else, British or American (for he was seeing American papers); it was up to them to decide what should be done with it. But as background, he passed on verbally the information that this was part of a project to build an atomic fission bomb, that the theoretical work on uranium diffusion was being supplemented by the construction of a model diffusion plant in Valley, Wales, that similar work was going on in the United States, and that there was collaboration between Britain and the United States in this.

**

This verbal background was probably the most important information Fuchs gave at this stage. For it arrived in the Soviet Union at a time when the Government was being pressed, as the British and American governments had been a little earlier, to take a decision on whether to go ahead with work on an atomic bomb.

Atomic physics was open and international until 1940. Russian scientists read all the papers that were published, and made substantial contributions of their own. They saw as soon as anyone else the possibilities of a nuclear chain reaction, and this was discussed openly. A few physicists were anxious to press ahead and explore the possibility, and in 1940 the Soviet Academy of Sciences set up a Uranium Commission, to plan further research and look for uranium ores. Igor Kurchatov, the head of nuclear physics at the Leningrad Physiotechnical Institute, along with a colleague, sent a proposal to the Academy for a programme of research leading to the construction of an experimental reactor, but the Academy decided that the prospect of results was too remote to justify such an expenditure.

Then Germany invaded, and even Kurchatov thought work on atomic fission would have to be shelved in favour of more urgent defence projects, and he went to work on protecting ships against magnetic mines. However, another physicist was able to work out that an atomic bomb programme was under way elsewhere, by a process that shows how difficult it is to switch from openness to secrecy. This was a younger colleague of Kurchatov called G. N. Flyorov, who was at that time a lieutenant in the Air Force. He was reading through the academic journals in his field, and he suddenly realized that after the flurry of excitement about nuclear fission in 1939 and 1940, no leading American or British physicist had published anything on the subject. Flyorov noticed the dog that did not bark. He concluded that work on atomic fission must now be secret. He wrote a letter to Stalin calling for an urgent programme to build a uranium bomb, and his letter was considered by the State Defence Committee.

Fuchs's information confirmed Flyorov's thesis. Soviet Intelligence also learned that German scientists were exploring the possibility of building a bomb, although this turned out to be only a very limited effort. Stalin himself was informed of all this.

The State Defence Committee put Mikhail Pervukhin, the Minister for the Chemical Industry, in charge of uranium research. Then in April 1942, as told at the beginning of this book, the Foreign Minister, Vyacheslav Molotov, on Stalin's personal instructions, gave Pervukhin a file containing foreign intelligence material, and told him to consult his scientists on what action to take. This file would have contained Fuchs's first reports to Kremer. Presumably the scientists also saw reports he sent later in the year; they evidently recommended the commencement of a bomb programme. At the end of the year the State Defence Committee ordered the establishment of a laboratory to work on a uranium bomb, with Kurchatov in charge, and work began the following March.

This was a remarkable commitment considering what must have been the urgent demands on scientific and other resources at that time. David Holloway, the Soviet affairs specialist who has made a study of the Soviet nuclear weapons programme, has written: 'The key factor in the atomic decision of 1942 was Soviet knowledge of the German and American work on the bomb.'[v]

The Maud Committee's work had spurred on the United States to put an atomic bomb project into gear. Thanks to Fuchs, it had much the same effect in the Soviet Union. The detailed papers that Fuchs passed over were read by scientists working in the field in Russia. This is evident from the fact that questions were sent to his contacts in Britain, who in turn passed them on to Fuchs. Most of the questions at this stage were either random shots in the dark, or else they were misinterpreted in transmission, because they made no sense to Fuchs. But one did: he was asked whether he knew anything about using electromagnetism to separate uranium 235. He was surprised, and said he did not know anything about this, which was true. But the Tube Alloys group in Oxford had made a preliminary examination of the possibility of this, and at the Berkeley laboratory in California, Ernest Lawrence was developing a serious electromagnetic separation project.

In 1942 Fuchs applied again for British citizenship. This time he had the backing of the Tube Alloys directorate, which said that, although an enemy alien, he was doing work that was valuable for the war effort. An application for citizenship must have two sponsors. One of his was Professor Nevill Mott, who, unlike his other mentors and friends, was British-born. Fuchs became a British citizen and took an oath of allegiance to the Crown on 7 August 1942. At this time, he was regularly passing secret information to the Soviet intelligence service. In America, naturalization is a part of the national story, the great step of becoming an American which nearly every one of their forefathers has passed through. It does not have the same significance for most people in Britain, and clearly Fuchs did not see his oath of allegiance as a constraint on his actions.

Early in 1942, several leading Tube Alloys scientists visited the United States to see the work being done there, as part of the programme of Anglo-American co-operation. Peierls was among them. There were hazards in crossing the Atlantic in wartime, and Peierls left instructions on the continuation of his work if he should be killed. The British scientists found that although they were ahead of the Americans on the theoretical side, the Americans had made great progress in experimental work, and were already working on three different possible methods of uranium diffusion.

Fuchs was forming friendships. He was becoming fond of the Peierls, and they of him. When he had a short holiday he went up to Edinburgh and stayed with Max Born and his wife. He became ill for a few days with a dry cough that was to continue to trouble him for some years, and sat in the Peierls' little garden, wrapped in a heavy woollen dressing-gown. The doctor who saw him took to him, and invited him home to dinner. Later, when the doctor was ill with leukaemia and Fuchs was in America, Fuchs sent him a food parcel.

The Peierls had their house on a five-year lease, which was to run out towards the end of 1942. They found a flat but there would be no room in it for a lodger. Mrs Peierls told Fuchs that he would have to find somewhere else to live. But he evidently found it hard to accept that he would have to leave the security of their home, and made no move to find another place even when the time for leaving the house drew closer. 'Klaus, you'll *have* to start looking for a place of your own,' Mrs Peierls would tell him. 'There won't be any room for you in our flat. It only has four rooms.' Only when they were about to move did he find a room in a boarding-house near their flat.

At the end of 1942 the Peierls gave a New Year's Eve party. Mrs Peierls had a lot to drink, and as she often did on such occasions she began to sing Russian songs. She suddenly noticed Fuchs gazing at her with a look of extraordinary intensity, such as she had never seen on him before, with an expression of what could have been adoration. It occurred to her that their young friend might be falling in love with her, and she made a mental note to discourage any such attachment. But there were no more signs of this, and she forgot the thought, although the intensity of Fuchs's gaze remained in her memory. Later, when Fuchs's activities were revealed, she decided that this look of adoration was directed, not at her, but at the reminder of Russia in the songs she was singing, a land that was the repository of his hopes for the world.

A degree of admiration for Russia was widespread in Britain at this time, and in America also. America and Britain were at war with Germany, but they were not yet engaged on any major front in Europe. The Russians were doing nearly all the fighting, and they were doing what no other country had succeeded in doing so far — halting the German army's advance and turning it back. The massive governmental aid to Russia was supplemented by private donations to Soviet war charities, sometimes raised in humble surroundings, sometimes at fund-raising banquets in the smartest American hotels.[vi] Max Born wrote in a letter to Fuchs, recalling their argument over the Soviet invasion of Finland in 1939: 'The news from Russia seems quite hopeful. You must be gratified that your belief in the Russians is so much justified now, even with respect to Finland.'

Fuchs had always kept his views secret. Now he was keeping from his new friends his activities also: his trips to Banbury, and his service to the Soviet state. But the country he was helping was a much-admired ally. He could believe that his friends might disapprove of what he was doing if

they knew, but would not be outraged; that they would only feel that he had broken some rules that, strictly speaking, he should not have broken, that he had gone too far in acting on a feeling towards Russia which, to some degree, they all shared.

Churchill and Roosevelt met in Quebec in August 1943 and signed a secret agreement on Anglo-American collaboration (along with Canada) on building an atomic bomb. The bomb would be built in America, and Britain would be a junior partner in the project. The Tube Alloys directorate recognized now that building the bomb would be a massive industrial undertaking, and this could not be done in Britain under wartime conditions.

The biggest single task would be separating uranium 235; British scientists had done a great deal of work on this and had a lot to contribute. So it was arranged that a group of British scientists would be attached to the team in New York working on uranium diffusion, and others would join other branches of the project.

Naturally, Peierls was asked to go to New York, and naturally, he asked Fuchs to come with him; Fuchs agreed. As it happens, Fuchs's name was known to the Americans working on uranium separation because he had written an excellent paper on the control of a particular problem in the diffusion process.

At this point, Fuchs could have let his activities as a Soviet informant drop. He had already given Russia some worthwhile help. His present contact was arranged through his own party, the German Communist Party, but now he was going away and the direct connection would be broken. However, he wanted to continue and he became even more involved; his espionage became more determined, the mechanics more complicated.

At his next meeting with Sonja, Fuchs told her that he was going to New York. She said she would arrange for him to be passed on to a contact in America. The GRU moved quickly, and when they met next she had details of the transfer. They were the stuff of spy fiction, with coded recognition signals. His contact in America would be a man he would know only as Raymond.

As a formality, he had to apply for a non-immigrant visa. On the form he wrote his occupation as 'government official', and the purpose of his visit as 'official duty on behalf of the Department of Scientific and Industrial Research'. (The DSIR had taken over the project from the Ministry of Aircraft Production.) The application is dated 22 November 1943.

The party of thirty British scientists and some of their wives sailed a few days after this, on the *Andes*. The crossing was very different from Fuchs's last journey to the New World. He was travelling as an official of the Government that three and a half years earlier had sent him across the Atlantic as a prisoner. He was travelling with friends, and sharing a stateroom with Otto Frisch. Although it was mid-winter, the sea was calm. The *Andes* was a cruise liner converted into a troop-ship, but only civilians were crossing the Atlantic in a westerly direction. There was plenty of food left over from the last crossing from America, so that the passengers, coming from a country where food was severely rationed and eggs limited to one a week, were treated to luxuries such as two eggs and bacon for breakfast every day, and meat and fresh fruit in abundance. They discussed their work, but in the main, people's memory of that crossing is of a short, relaxed interlude, during which they put on weight.

***

Fuchs never played tennis but, late in the afternoon of a crisp, cold Saturday in February 1944, he was strolling along Henry Street, on the lower East Side of Manhattan, carrying a tennis ball. He was following the instructions that Sonja had given him. The tennis ball was to be the sign by which Raymond, his American espionage contact, would recognize him.

Fuchs saw what he was watching out for: a man wearing gloves and carrying another pair of gloves in his hand, and carrying also a book with a green cover. He was in his mid-thirties, shortish, with a pallid complexion and pudgy features, and large, soulful eyes and heavy eyelids almost hidden behind thick-lensed glasses.

As instructed, Fuchs waited for the other to make the first approach and he did so, with the expected question: 'Can you tell me the way to Grand Central Station?' Fuchs shrugged this off with a non-committal reply, and the other said something meaningless. There was a pause; they had both given the right signals.

'Raymond?' said Fuchs, and the other nodded. Fuchs introduced himself.

Raymond said he was pleased to meet Fuchs, and pleased to have been chosen for such an important assignment. They walked along together, Fuchs telling him a little about his work in New York and the atomic bomb project, of which the American, in common with most other people, had never heard. They made arrangements for further meetings, with an eye to tight security. They would meet only briefly, allowing just enough time to complete their business. They would never meet in the same place twice. And at each meeting they would make arrangements for the next one, including a time and place. They parted after twenty minutes.

Raymond — and Fuchs never knew him by any other name — was Harry Gold, one of the strangest figures to feature in a major espionage case. In fact he featured in two, because he was to be a key witness in the case against Julius and Ethel Rosenberg, the couple who became an international *cause célèbre* in the early 1950s when they were sentenced to death for spying for the Soviet Union.

A native of Philadelphia, he came from a poor background but worked his way through college and earned a degree in chemistry. He worked for a chemical company and a hospital laboratory, and from 1936 onwards, according to his own account, he passed confidential information about industrial chemical processes gathered from his places of work to Soviet agents. He had high blood pressure and was unfit for military service. A bachelor, he lived with his parents in Philadelphia.

He had two major eccentricities, both reflecting social inadequacy, which make him an improbable agent of a serious espionage organization.

He was a fantasist, who created stories about himself for their own sake. For instance, he told investigators that his Soviet contact advised him to tell his employers that he was married in order to make himself more acceptable, which in itself seems unlikely. He not only said he was married, but invented detailed storied about his wife's former lover, in-law troubles, buying a house, and finally a break-up of the marriage which left him deprived of his children (a boy and a girl, twins) and racked with anguish at the loss. He told friends the heart-rending story of how he would sit in his car outside his children's school and wait for them to come out, and watch them from a distance, and cry silently. He would sometimes break down in tears as he told this story, and the friends listening would be near to tears also. Another story of his family life, which has an obvious unconscious motivation, was that his younger brother, Joe, was in the army and had been killed in action in the Pacific. Gold did have a younger brother called Joe and it would be natural for him to be jealous of him, for as a boy Joe was athletic and popular, in contrast to Gold; he was serving in the army and had been decorated. In the arguments that have gone on about the Rosenberg case since their execution, one of the points put forward in favour of their innocence is Gold's apparent unreliability as a witness.

The other eccentricity was a desire to please which went to extraordinary lengths. As a student, Gold used to help others with their work to the detriment of his own. He was always eager to perform a service for someone else, no matter how inconvenient. He would lend money to anyone, even when he was in financial difficulties himself and in debt, and when the borrower paid him back he always had to argue with Gold to get him to accept the money. He was an ideal employee, doing more than was asked of him and always ready to do any amount of overtime work. When he himself was placed on trial for espionage, his defence counsel told the judge: 'Harry Gold is the most extraordinarily selfless person I have ever met in my life.' But Gold's behaviour was not simply selfless: it was pathologically self-abnegating.

It appears to be this trait that led Gold to agree to the suggestion of someone he met that he hand over confidential information from the laboratory where he worked to be passed on to the Soviet Union. Seeking to explain this later, he said he did it at first out of gratitude to someone who helped him get a job, and later out of sympathy for the Russian people. He seems to have had no Communist convictions (he was a registered Democrat) and he was not paid for his services. He was just a man who could not say 'No'.

After 1941 Gold had no useful information to give, and he acted as a courier for a Soviet official, collecting papers for him at various times in secret. In February 1944, this official told him that he was to drop everything else he was doing for him and take on some work that was very important, and that he must keep this absolutely secret. This was to begin when he met a visitor from England in downtown Manhattan.

Fuchs had arrived with the others on the *Andes* on 3 December, landing at Newport News, Virginia. The ones who were going to New York left by train right away. They were paid a living allowance which for Fuchs, as a bachelor, meant a substantial rise in his standard of living. On his arrival in New York, he went with most of the others to stay at the Taft Hotel near Times Square, and then moved to the Barbizon Plaza, a comfortable and fairly elegant hotel in a smart location overlooking Central Park. After two months there, he rented a furnished apartment at 128 West 77th Street, in a four-storey converted brownstone house. He took it over from another scientist with the British mission who was returning to England.

In every way, life seemed to be getting better for Fuchs. Soon after his arrival he had a reunion with his younger sister, Kristel. She was married to a man called Robert Heineman, who had an income derived partly from a small business he owned. They lived in a neat suburban-style house in Cambridge, Massachusetts, and had two children, a boy of three and a one-year-old girl. Fuchs spent Christmas with the Heinemans. Heineman told friends that he found Fuchs stand-offish, but he made him welcome in his home, and Fuchs went up to visit them twice more during his stay in New York.

Quite apart from anyone having more money, life in New York was much more abundant than life in wartime Birmingham. There was some rationing in America, and a 'brown-out' in coastal cities which restricted street-lighting, but compared to any British city at this time, where life was austere and the streets were blacked out at night, New York was a glittering cornucopia of food and drink and the material good things of life. People had money to spend and the city thronged with servicemen on leave. The Broadway theatre was flourishing. Restaurants and night-clubs were packed. But somehow, all this did not make a great impression on most of the British scientists, who were preoccupied with the work they had come to do.

For the war overseas was in the minds of most people in America, and probably more prominently in the minds of the British visitors, who had come from a war zone. In the newspapers and on the radio the constant news for Americans was of other Americans struggling and dying, and, by 1944, purchasing victories with their suffering. It was of Allied servicemen inching their way painfully up the Italian peninsula, fighting terrible battles against well-dug-in Japanese troops on one Pacific island after another, dying in the sky in the massive air raids on German cities, and then, in June of that year, wading ashore in Normandy to begin the liberation of Europe. Much of the attention of the people back home was focused on these men and what they were doing. People tried to help, by buying war bonds, or giving blood.

The scientists working on the atomic bomb were engaged in the same titanic effort, and they were aware that they might be able to shorten the war and the suffering. It was not only a question of shortening the war; they knew what the newspaper-reading public did not know: that the possibility of an atomic bomb existed, and that German scientists might somehow produce one.

Fuchs liked music and occasionally went to a concert, usually alone. He had acquired a violin, and sometimes played. He also went out with a few others and climbed on the Pallisades, the cliffs in New Jersey facing New York across the river. He liked climbing. Apart from this, he had little recreation.

The Peierls brought their young son and daughter from Toronto to live with them. Their daughter Gaby, reunited with her parents at the age of twelve after an absence of two and a half years, was quiet and withdrawn for a while, so that her mother said, 'Oh, she's just like Klaus.' So Gaby was curious to meet Fuchs. When she did she took to him, and came to like him more over the years. He paid attention to her, and she found quickly that he was kind, in a quiet way.

The fifteen scientists in the Tube Alloys team in-New York came under the aegis of the British Ministry of Supply, and they worked in a set of offices taken by the Ministry in Exchange Place, near Wall Street. The theoretical work on uranium diffusion had been done at Columbia University, and the theory was now being put into practice with the construction of a huge uranium separation plant at Oak Ridge, Tennessee, which in terms of cost and manpower was to be the biggest part of the atomic bomb programme. Its location was a secret even from the scientists working on diffusion in New York. These were doing mathematical calculations in connection with the plant, which was being built by the Kellex Corporation, a corporation created just for this task by Kellogg's, the big engineering firm.

Most of the Britons went home in the early months of 1944 but Peierls and Fuchs remained, and also another assistant of Peierls who had come with them from Birmingham, Tony Skyrme. Skyrme was younger than Fuchs and had an Eton and Oxford background and the kind of English accent that goes with it. This accent was so pronounced, and so alien to Americans, that when he went for a walk in Central Park in his shirtsleeves one warm evening without any papers on him, he was arrested and told by police that they suspected him of being a Nazi spy. This was something that never happened to any of the German-born members of the British mission. All the Britons who remained were listed officially as consultants to the Kellex Corporation.

As Fuchs was foreign-born, one of the directors of Tube Alloys asked M15 at this point for a summary of anything that was known about him, since it was proposed now that he should remain in America working with the Americans. MI5 reported that he had not been active politically and there was nothing objectionable about his behaviour in Britain.

One of the American scientists involved in the diffusion project in New York was Edward Corson, Fuchs's old friend from Edinburgh, but somehow they did not see much of each other out of working hours.

At one point, Peierls encountered a difficulty of an unexpected kind. The British group wanted to hire someone locally to help with some mathematical calculations and he called Hunter College, a college in New York (a university by British standards), that was then a women-only institution. The Hunter office said they would send along a young woman who was black (the word used in those days was 'coloured'): would this present a problem? Peierls consulted a senior official at the Ministry of Supply office in New York, who said that some people might object if he hired a coloured girl. However, this person said that in order not to offend American anti-discrimination laws he should interview the girl and then turn her down. Peierls was angry at this but decided that making an issue of it would interfere with work on the project, which was of overriding importance. However, he refused to practise deception, and told Hunter College that he was not allowed to hire a black girl.

He told the story to Fuchs and, knowing that Fuchs had high principles, he expected him to say that he should have taken a strong stand against a colour bar. But Fuchs said he thought he did the right thing, and that it was better to pursue the greater good of uninterrupted work on the bomb project, which might win the war.

Fuchs was also pursuing another goal, of giving the Soviet Union whatever help he could in building an atomic bomb. Most of what he was able to pass on was his own work, but he was no longer restricting himself to this as a matter of principle, as he had before. One factor may have been that he believed what the British and American Communist Parties were saying: that Britain and America were deliberately holding back from invading Europe in order that Germany and Russia might bleed each other to death. In Britain, a 'second front now' campaign was mounted, with mass meetings and demonstrations.

He met Gold again about two weeks after their first encounter, at the corner of 59th Street and Lexington Avenue. This was not the peremptory meeting they had decided they would have. It was in the evening, like all their meetings, and they walked across to First Avenue, and then up-town for fifteen blocks or so.

Fuchs had no papers to hand over yet, but he talked about the uranium diffusion programme and its place in the atomic bomb project. He told Gold that two methods of separating the isotopes of uranium were being pursued, gaseous diffusion and electromagnetic separation. He noted that Gold had some scientific knowledge — he seems to have known about isotope separation, for instance — and guessed he might be a chemist. He also told Gold about the members of the British group working in New York, and about some of the Americans as well. Gold was diligent: he kept this in his mind and wrote it all down as soon as he had left Fuchs. He had acquired a new controller, whom he knew only as John. This was Anatoli Yakovlev, whose official post was Soviet vice-consul in New York. Gold gave Yakovlev his written report of his conversations with Fuchs. Gold used to come up from Philadelphia, a journey of about two and a half hours by train, for these meetings.

The third meeting, two weeks after this one, was strictly business. Fuchs and Gold met by arrangement among the smart, busy, illuminated shops of Madison Avenue in the 70s, and turned down a side street. This time Fuchs handed over an envelope containing several pages, and they made arrangements for the next meeting. That was all.

At the next meeting, they broke all the rules they had set for themselves. They met outside a cinema in the Bronx. It was a chilly, damp evening in April, rain was coming down, and Fuchs had a bad cough. Gold was worried about Fuchs being out in this weather, so at his insistence they went to a nearby restaurant and had dinner. Fuchs told Gold that a big uranium diffusion plant was being built somewhere in the South, possibly Georgia or Alabama. Over dinner, they talked about music and chess. Co-conspirators now, they agreed on a story in case anyone should ask how they met: they would say that they happened to be sitting next to each other at a concert at Carnegie Hall and got to chatting. Gold was even going to go home and look up the Carnegie Hall concert programme in a newspaper so that he would know what was played on a particular day and could make the story convincing.

After dinner, they took a taxi into Manhattan and went to a mid-town bar, and had some drinks. Then they left in two separate cabs, Fuchs for home, Gold for Pennsylvania Station.

Fuchs handed over an envelope before they parted.

It must have been a curious evening. Gold never revealed his identity, and Fuchs, knowing that 'Raymond' was merely a *nom de guerre,* disdained to use it. Gold addressed Fuchs as 'Klaus'. But Fuchs, who rarely talked about his family even to close friends, talked about his brother to this stranger. He had received a letter from his brother Gerhardt, and he told Gold about Gerhardt's flight to Switzerland, and his poor health. Gold, always eager to be a friend, listened appreciatively.

***

They met next in the suburb of Queens, and this time it was strictly business again. Fuchs handed over a bulky envelope containing somewhere between twenty-five and forty pages, and Gold took it to Yakovlev. He arrived a few minutes early for his street-corner meeting with Yakovlev, and, curious, he opened the envelope and glanced at the material inside by the light of a drugstore window. He saw pages of handwriting with mathematical derivations, which he did not understand.

These, like all the written material that Fuchs handed over, were reports that he had written himself. He wrote thirteen papers on uranium diffusion while he was attached to the Kellex Company in New York, and he gave copies of every one to Gold. At the office on Exchange Place Fuchs used to write out a draft of each paper in longhand, including the mathematical calculations, and give it to a secretary to type and duplicate, sometimes showing it to Peierls first for approval. The typed and duplicated copies were numbered first for security purposes. A copy was given to him to check, along with the handwritten original, and this copy also would be numbered. He would keep the copy, and give the handwritten original to Gold.

They were highly technical, with titles such as *Fluctuations and the Efficiency of a Diffusion Plant,* Parts 1-4, and *On the Effect of a Time Lag in the Control of Plant Stability.* They were useful in the construction of a uranium diffusion plant in America, and presumably would be useful to the Russians as they made plans to construct one.

The security regulations covering the handling of documents were not as tight as they were to be later on. Some of the scientists would take classified documents home to work on them. One recalls that he was told simply never to let these out of his possession, so that when he stopped at an art museum on the way home one day, he had to refuse to surrender his briefcase at the cloakroom, and was not allowed in.

A little while after the meeting in Queens, Fuchs went on another visit to the Heinemans. He found Kristel very troubled. Her marriage was often unhappy; one quarrel on the street was so violent that the police were called. Now she was thinking of leaving her husband and moving to New York with her two children.

Then he showed how strong was his commitment to his role as a Soviet informant. When he met Gold next, near Borough Hall in Brooklyn, he told him about his sister, and said that if she did leave her husband and come to New York, he would like to share an apartment with her. He said he was very close to his sister, and fond of her two children. But first he wanted Gold to ask his superiors whether there would be any objection to this arrangement.

Some more questions about Fuchs's reports came back, evidently from scientists in the Soviet Union. Before this meeting, Yakovlev gave Gold several small sheets of paper with typewritten questions on them. Gold read them and found it difficult to make sense out of them, mainly because they were phrased in stilted English, like a bad translation. He did not give the questions to Fuchs but relayed them as best he could. At least, he started to relay them, but Fuchs said brusquely that he had already covered all these matters thoroughly, and would continue to do so.

The Soviet programme was not yet in high gear, but plans were being laid and Fuchs's data were being used. When the Soviet uranium diffusion plant was built at Podolsk, just south of Moscow, it was an exact copy of the plant at Oak Ridge, Tennessee.

Fuchs and Gold met next at the Metropolitan Museum on Fifth Avenue, and because it was a warm evening they strolled in Central Park for a while. Gold told Fuchs that there would be no objection to his sharing an apartment with his sister. He had not consulted anyone before giving this reply, but took it upon himself. In fact, Kristel was not going to leave her husband now; she was pregnant. A third child was born in October of that year.

While they walked, Fuchs told him a few more titbits that he had picked up about the Manhattan Project, as the atomic bomb project was now called. He told him that Niels Bohr, one of the giants of twentieth-century science, had joined it. He had been smuggled out of German-occupied Denmark to Sweden, and had now been brought to the United States under the name Nicholas Baker, as Fuchs informed Gold. Fuchs also told him an item of news about himself: he said he expected to be transferred away from New York to somewhere in the south-western United States later in the year or early the following year. He gave him his sister Kristel's address, and said that if they lost contact he could leave a message for him there.

He explained that work on the Manhattan Project was compartmentalized, so that no one knew much about what was going on in other branches. He gave Gold another envelope just before they parted. If they spent some time together, he would always wait until the last moment before handing over the papers, so that if they were caught together Gold would not have classified papers on him.

During some of this time Fuchs was sharing an office at

Exchange Place with Nicholas Kurd, a dapper Hungarian physicist and *bon vivant* who had worked for Tube Alloys at Oxford, and they became friends. Kurd was one of the first to notice Fuchs's growing concern with security. Several atomic scientists knew that the writer Harold Nicolson had made an uncannily accurate forecast of an atomic bomb (although purely by chance) in a novel published in 1934, *Public Faces,* Fuchs was distressed to find it in the little library at the Barbizon Plaza, among the books available to residents. 'Couldn't the book somehow be taken out of circulation?' he asked Kurti anxiously.

Kurd's view of him at this time is interesting. Their friendship was limited: Kurti did not feel that he could overcome Fuchs's reserve sufficiently to have an intimate relationship with him. But he says he saw in him a rare quality of integrity. As he explains: 'I somehow had the feeling that if I got into difficulties of some kind, I could go to him for advice, and could be absolutely certain that he would not betray my trust, and that he would do everything he could to help me.' Nothing that has happened since has altered Kurd's view.

What Kurti sensed were Fuchs's decent instincts which were beginning to come through in his responses to other people, and also the integrity he learned from his father, the same integrity that was leading him now to the removal of confidential papers and secret meetings with Gold.

Fuchs was by now operating on two planes which were quite separate from one another, the political and the personal. He was being, more and more, a caring friend and an honest one, albeit with a certain emotional reserve; but on a political level he was committing acts of betrayal. He was like the married man who carries on an affair while telling himself that he still loves his wife, and that the affair has nothing to do with her and does not affect their relationship.

The moat between his emotional life and other people which

he had dug when he left Germany was still there, but he had thrown bridges across it. He was developing human ties, human friendships, and expressing human decencies, things he had given up when he left his homeland for a strange country and withdrew behind his defences.

He described years later, in his confession, the process that was clearly well established by this time:

> In the course of this work I began naturally to form bonds of personal friendship... I used my Marxist philosophy to establish in my mind two separate compartments. One compartment in which I allowed myself to make friendships, to have personal relations, to help people and to be in all personal ways the kind of man I wanted to be and the kind of man which, in personal ways, I had been before with my friends in or near the Communist Party. I could be free and easy and happy with other people without fear of disclosing myself because I knew that the other compartment would step in if I approached the danger point. I could forget the other compartment and still rely on it. It appeared to me at the time that I had become a 'free man', because I had succeeded in the other compartment to establish myself completely independent of the surrounding forces in society. Looking back at it now the best way of expressing it seems to be to call it a controlled schizophrenia.[vii]

The confession was written in 1950, and that phrase 'a free man' seems to echo the existentialist literature of the time (although it is unlikely that there was a direct literary influence: Fuchs did not read a great deal outside his professional field). The kind of freedom he describes is emotional autonomy, an absence of any obligations or commitments imposed by the social environment, or by ties to others, or by other people's expectations. It is the freedom of Albert Camus's *Outsider,* and of the psychopath. It is quite un-Marxist. The Marxist views man as being first and foremost a social animal, and would regard the state of being 'independent of the surrounding forces of society' as being neither possible nor desirable.

It is also interesting that when he describes himself as having been helpful and a friend in the past, it was with other people 'in or near the Communist Party'. Friendship still seemed inseparable from political alignment.

Fuchs had the necessary mental equipment of a spy: the emotional self-reliance, the ability to do without the approval of others, the ability to live on two planes at once, being one thing on one plane and quite a different thing on the other. One thinks of Kim Philby, who was a husband, lover, hard drinker and a valued and highly competent British intelligence agent, and was also, in a part of his life known to none of his friends and colleagues, an agent of the KGB. It was fortuitous that Fuchs had this ability. For Fuchs, unlike Kim Philby, unlike George Blake, the other double agent in the British intelligence service, and several Americans who were found more recently to have served the KGB, did not set out to be a spy. He became one by chance, simply because he came across some very important information, because, in fact, he was a physicist at a time when the application of physics turned out to be the most important thing happening in the world.

Fuchs's next meeting with Gold after their stroll in Central Park was to be outside the Bell movie theatre in Brooklyn, in July. Fuchs did not turn up. This was the first meeting he had missed. Gold reported this to Yakovlev and returned to Philadelphia. He went to the next alternative rendezvous a short time later, on Central Park West in the 90s, and again Fuchs did not appear. This was a high crime area, and Gold was worried that Fuchs might have been mugged.

In espionage, unlike most other crimes, there is very rarely an act of violence or theft. The crime is the transmission of information. Often, the crime is perpetrated simply by the meeting of two people. Such a meeting may point to the crime, and so the spy goes to great lengths to keep secret the links in the chain which lead from the source of the information to the ultimate receiver. Gold could not simply telephone Fuchs to ask why he had not turned up and when they could meet, since this might attract suspicion. Fuchs had never even told him his address. Two failed meetings in a row meant a severing of contact.

He reported back to Yakovlev and they had a long discussion, going over various possibilities. Yakovlev went away to consult a superior or else think it over. They met again on a Sunday morning near Washington Square. Yakovlev told Gold that he now had Fuchs's address, and he told him to go to the apartment.

Now Gold showed ingenuity. The bookstall at Grand Central Station was open on Sunday mornings, so he went there and bought a recently published novel by Thomas Mann. Then he wrote in the inside cover: 'K. Fuchs, 128 West 77th Street, New York, NY'. He went to the brownstone house at that address and rang Fuchs's bell. He got no answer, so he went to the janitor. He told him he was a friend of Fuchs, and had come to return this book that Fuchs had loaned him. The janitor told him only that Fuchs no longer lived there, and said he had gone away 'somewhere on a boat'. Gold went to report back to Yakovlev.

The Russian was waiting for him on upper Broadway, standing on a street corner among the people coming out to buy their huge Sunday newspapers or some fresh bagels or platzels for a Sunday brunch. The two men walked down to Riverside Drive and strolled along in the sunshine discussing what they could do next. The only thing now seemed to be to wait to hear from Fuchs and, if they did not hear from him, to leave a message with his sister in Cambridge. Yakovlev told Gold, in a colloquial English he had evidently acquired, 'Sit tight'.

Gold went back to Philadelphia. The next month, September, he took a bus to Boston one Sunday, arriving there in the evening. He went to the Heinemans' house and knocked on the door. A woman answered and said the Heinemans were away on vacation and would not be back until sometime in October.

He went back to Yakovlev, and they agreed that he should make another trip later. Yakovlev suggested that he go on a weekday, when Robert Heineman was not likely to be at home. Yakovlev also gave him a message, which Gold typed out. This told Fuchs to telephone a certain number any day between 8.00 and 8.30, and say simply, 'I have arrived in Cambridge and will be here for — days.' He put this in an envelope and sealed it. He went up to Cambridge on a weekday in early November and knocked on the door, and this time Mrs Heineman answered.

Gold said he was a good friend of Fuchs from New York, and had lost touch with him; he happened to be in the Boston area on business and thought he would stop by and inquire after him. He said Fuchs had given him her address. Mrs Heineman told him that she expected him there at Christmas. Gold gave her the envelope for Fuchs. She said he had been transferred to another place; she did not know where it was, except that it was somewhere in the south-western United States.

CHAPTER THREE

One morning in November 1942, when Peierls and Fuchs were working in Birmingham on the Tube Alloys programme, two American physicists, Robert Oppenheimer and Edwin McMillan, rode on horseback into the Jemez Mountains, in the northern part of New Mexico. They were riding through some of the most magnificent scenery in the North American continent, but at this time of year it was cold at higher altitudes, and light snow flurries accompanied them some of the way, the snowflakes making the horses' hooves slip as they melted underfoot, and adding a wet glisten to their flanks. However, Oppenheimer and McMillan were not riding for recreation; they were exploring.

They were both engaged in theoretical physics work on the atomic bomb project at the University of California's campus at Berkeley. Their ride into the mountains followed a decision that a new laboratory should be created at which work on the atomic bomb would be carried through. It was decided that this laboratory should not be built at one of the places where work on the bomb was going on already — Columbia, the University of Chicago and Berkeley — but at an entirely new location. The site should be remote, in order that the work could be secret and secure, but there should be at least one good road leading to it so that equipment could be brought up. Oppenheimer owned a ranch in this part of New Mexico along with his brother Frank, and he thought that a place meeting all these requirements might be found there.

On this particular morning, they were going to look at a canyon that he and Major-General Leslie Groves, who was in overall command of the atomic bomb project, had picked out on a map. They rode down into it but decided that there was not enough space, and the canyon walls would be too confining. When Groves arrived in his staff car to meet them in the afternoon, Oppenheimer told him this. However, he said, he knew another site nearby which might be suitable: a place called Los Alamos, where there was now a boys' school. They tethered their mounts and drove there with Groves in his car, and this time they liked what they saw. They talked to the school principal, who was also the owner. It turned out that the school did not have enough pupils and had fallen on hard times, and he would be only too happy to sell the land to the Government. Groves sent a telegram to Washington, and negotiations for the purchase of Los Alamos began immediately.

The laboratory that was established there in the spring of 1943, a place where Fuchs was to spend nearly two years, was the most extraordinary scientific centre there has ever been. More eminent scientists went to work there than have ever gathered in any other place for a prolonged period of time, taking leave of the academic world to vanish behind a wire fence. They were highly motivated, and worked with a dedication and a spirit of comradeship that made the years there, for most of them, one of the peak experiences of their lives. The atmosphere was very democratic. For the younger men, just out of university, one of the things that made the place exciting was that they were working and living alongside some of the giants in their field, whose discoveries they had only recently been learning about.

The entire laboratory and living area was a military base, and everyone there lived under military jurisdiction, in homes built by the army. They had to get permission from the army to be away overnight, and all incoming and outgoing mail was censored. Since the existence of the laboratory was a secret, they could give their address only as Box 1663, Santa Fe. They had no legal residence, and therefore could not vote. Even the Los Alamos troop of the Boy Scouts of America was anonymous; it was not allowed to send to the Boy Scouts' national headquarters the names of scouts who had won badges, as is customary, because their names might reveal the presence of their scientist fathers.

The community was an isolated one: by geography, for there was no town closer than Santa Fe, thirty miles away; by the strict secrecy that surrounded the work; and also by the esoteric nature of the work, which bound together the people doing it. For the scientists, being at Los Alamos meant working harder than most of them had ever worked before, wrestling with the many problems of using nuclear physics to create an explosive device: a fourteen-hour day was not uncommon, and a six-day working week was the established norm. It meant spending much of what leisure time they had in the company of the same people with whom they spent their working hours, and most of these people becoming friends, special friends. For the wives, it meant exchanging advice on acquiring food from the army's stores and cooking on their wood-burning stoves. It also meant occasionally arguing with military and civilian clerks over the allocation of facilities, and when the army started bussing in Indian women from the surrounding area to serve as cleaners and part-time maids, for an allocation of some of their time. For everyone it meant parties at which they would dance to records and play party games, including a form of charades that became a favourite, called Indications. It meant trips out into the vastness of the countryside in an effort to put the pressure of the work behind them for a day or so with outdoor pursuits: hiking, riding, swimming in a nearby reservoir, skiing.

The scenery was an essential part of the Los Alamos experience. It is spectacularly beautiful: a sand-coloured landscape riven by winding canyons thousands of feet deep, the biggest of them containing the upper stretch of the Rio Grande, interspersed with mesas — narrow, steep-sided plateaus characteristic of the region, as if some giant god had doodled in wet sand with a mile-long forefinger. Soft rock faces have been sculpted by aeons of wind into outlandish shapes, and burnished in different colours. It is a landscape familiar to everyone from western films: the Indians on their horses at the cliff's edge, looking down on the stagecoach winding along the trail far below.

There are forests of fir, and ponderosa pine, and aspens that turn golden in the autumn; and forty miles to the west, but standing out sharply in the clean air, the Sangre de Cristo Mountains, so named by the Spanish explorers of this area because of the glorious blood-red glow along the peaks as the sun sets behind them. The air at Los Alamos is pure, and thin also, for it is 7,200 feet high.

Mrs Peierls recalled later being driven along the road up from Santa Fe on her arrival: 'It was late in the afternoon, the sun was low in the sky, and the colours were unbelievable! As we got higher and higher along this winding road, there were more cliffs at every turning, and forests, and long views, and sharply etched colours. It was just like climbing up to heaven!'

She added that this visual paradise came to an end when they arrived and she saw the ugly buildings that the army had put up. For in those days Los Alamos was a blot on this beautiful landscape. There were a few log cabins left over from the ranch school, but mostly one saw drab houses painted army green that looked like miniature barracks, and even more drab Nissen huts, and structures built to house machinery that provided the services, often of corrugated iron. The roads were merely tracks, dusty, or muddy if there had been rain or snow, some of them covered with duckboard, usually spanned at some point by a cluster of electric wires, or else clotheslines hung with washing.

Everyone was working there under the intense pressure of world events. They saw the prospect of shortening by their efforts the war that was costing thousands of lives every day, but also the nightmare possibility that Nazi Germany might beat them and get the bomb first.

By the summer of 1944, the uranium diffusion plant at Oak Ridge, Tennessee, was operating and the theoretical work in New York was finished. It was suggested that as Peierls, Fuchs and Skyrme already knew about the fundamentals of the bomb project they should go to Los Alamos and contribute their skills there, instead of returning to Britain. They agreed readily, and arrived in August. Several British scientists were already there. Otto Frisch had gone straight to Los Alamos after arriving from England on the *Andes,* as had a few others. James Chadwick, who had worked on Tube Alloys at Liverpool University, was designated chief of the British atomic energy mission in the United States, and had taken up residence there.

The project was divided into several divisions, and the three newcomers all joined the Theoretical Division, which was headed by the German-born Hans Bethe. Bethe had asked particularly for Peierls to come to Los Alamos. They had been warm friends ever since they were graduate students together in Munich in 1927, and found they shared the same sense of humour, and Bethe had a high regard for Peierls's ability. Bethe also had lived in the Peierls' house when he went to England from Germany in 1934. Although genial and friendly (his students at Cornell call him by his first name) he has the slow, slightly pedantic manner that one expects of a traditional German professor, but also one of the most powerful minds in modern physics. At a party at Los Alamos once, Frisch threw a complicated mathematical problem at Bethe and Richard Feynman, a brilliant, fast-talking young American physicist with a lightning manner (games like this were often played at Los Alamos parties). The betting was on the quicksilver Feynman, but Bethe solved it first.

Bethe recalled meeting Fuchs when he went to Bristol University for a short period in 1934, soon after leaving Germany. He remembered him, as he said later, as being 'brilliant, quiet and unassuming', and he agreed readily when Peierls said he wanted to bring him. At Los Alamos, he was confirmed in his high regard for Fuchs's abilities. But meeting him socially he could not get close to him, and found him inscrutable.

The Peierls found a number of old friends at Los Alamos, for there were many there from the international fraternity of young nuclear physicists of the 1930s. They were assigned the top half of a two-storey house; the bottom half was occupied by the Fermis, whom they had known when Peierls worked at Enrico Fermi's laboratory in Rome. Their children played together and became friends.

Fuchs was assigned a room in the big house that was used as bachelor quarters. He used to eat his meals with the other bachelors in Fuller's Lodge, the main administrative building and one that remained from the boarding school, where there was a communal dining-room.

There was nowhere to go in the evenings, and although people occasionally made the trip into Santa Fe, social life consisted mainly of visiting one another's homes, negotiating the duckboard avenues and the muddy paths in the dark, for there was no street lighting. The Peierls took Fuchs along when old friends asked them over, but in any case people were happy to invite this newcomer from England. He always accepted the invitations but, certainly at first, he showed his old reticence. The first evening he visited Martin and Suzanne Deutsch, he sat on the corner of a sofa facing a wall and did not say a word for hours on end. Nevertheless, they persisted in cultivating his friendship. For one thing, Deutsch, who came from Vienna, was impressed by the fact that Fuchs was a refugee because of his convictions rather than his race.

Genia Peierls organized a picnic for her family, the Fermis and Fuchs: she was a great one for organizing people. They drove to Frijoles Canyon some twenty miles away, a favourite spot for outings where the remains of prehistoric settlements and cave dwellings are to be found. Fuchs did not open up. He was nervous, and unresponsive to the Fermis' conversational overtures, and they did not get to know him well.

He got along better with Victor Weisskopf, a leading figure in the Theoretical Division. Unlike many others from Germany and Austria, who made every effort to become American or British to the point of losing their former national identities, the Viennese-born Weisskopf, a man with a wide appreciation of the arts, was determined to retain and even to assert his cultural heritage; he often spoke German at home with his Danish-born wife Ellen. Fuchs spoke German in the Weisskopfs' home, and on one occasion borrowed a German novel from them.

Fuchs became friendly with someone who could not be more unlike him in temperament, Richard Feynman, the fast-talking American who was bested by Bethe in the race to solve a mathematical problem. Feynman is today one of the great figures of physics, a Nobel laureate who devised space-time diagrams that are named after him. At Los Alamos he was still in his early twenties, a bubbling, excitable, irrepressible extrovert. He would play the bongo drums at parties, and do impersonations. He would tease soldiers on guard duty by checking out at the gate, crawling back in under the wire fence, and checking out again without having checked in. He used to sneak into people's offices and crack the locks of their combination safes, and leave jokey little notes inside. His method of cracking their safes eluded them: he guessed that many scientists would not bother to remember new numbers and would choose as the combinations of their safes scientific constants; one was simply pi backwards.

Fuchs and Feynman had adjoining rooms in the bachelors' building, sharing a bathroom, and sometimes they used to talk late into the night. Feynman used to tease Fuchs about his reticence. More earnestly, he urged him to come out of his shell, and suggested that he take out some girls, for there were a few young single women at Los Alamos. Once they had a light-hearted conversation about spies, and about which of them was a more likely suspect as a Nazi spy (which was the only kind that anyone was thinking about). Fuchs said it would be Feynman because of his frequent trips to Albuquerque, seventy miles away, and Feynman agreed. These trips were to visit his wife. For the clowning, fun-loving Feynman was living in the shadow of tragedy: his wife, whom he had married a few months earlier, was dying of tuberculosis in an Albuquerque hospital.

Among Americans, Fuchs's reserve was even more conspicuous than it had been in Britain, and it was remarked upon. Mrs Peierls's penny-in-the-slot description circulated. Wives talked about him, as they always will about a single man. When two of the wives were discussing him, Eleanor Jette summed up the negative impression he made on her: 'That guy baffles me. I can't remember what he looks like until the next time I see him.'

And Marjorie Schreiber said: 'He gives me the creeps. He sits in a corner at parties and never says a word. I've never heard him laugh: he has a high-pitched giggle, and it gives me the chills.'

Her hostility was unusual. Another wife described him as 'a sweet, reticent little guy'. Fuchs's silences seemed sad, and a lot of people felt vaguely sorry for him. Oppenheimer remarked once that he seemed to be carrying the weight of the world on his shoulders. There was still that barrier across his mind, and behind it lay that other compartment, which contained his commitment to help the Soviet Union, and who knows what else besides among his emotional baggage.

To some, the barrier seemed almost palpable. The Deutschs were convinced that there was another person behind the Fuchs they knew, and they discussed this between themselves. Martin Deutsch was the son of the well-known Viennese psychoanalyst Helen Deutsch, and they often discussed people in psychoanalytic terms. Edward Teller liked him, but also felt that there was something hidden back there; he found him, he said once, 'taciturn to an almost pathological degree'.

Yet during his time at Los Alamos Fuchs loosened up a little, as he became respected for his work and absorbed into the camaraderie of the place. He danced at parties. At Bristol, Lovell had remarked that he looked as if he never breathed fresh air, but now he sought pleasures in the outdoors, as many others did there. He used to go with others on day-long hikes, sometimes into the mountains. Occasionally, when the others were resting, he would show off his energy and skill by climbing a rock face at the side of the path, grinning at the achievement. When he climbed, his emotional self-control was matched by physical self-control. He went skiing, which he had not done since he was a student in Germany.

He may have been thin and slightly built, but he was not weak. There is a strong daytime sun at Los Alamos for seven or eight months of the year, although the air is thin and dry so that the nights are usually chilly. Fuchs acquired a healthy-looking outdoor tan, and the tautness was not so visible.

He bought a second-hand car, the only kind that could be had during the war, a four-door Buick. Many people at Los Alamos did not have cars, and he was often being asked to give people lifts or run errands, and he was nearly always willing. (Feynman borrowed his car to drive into Albuquerque when his wife died in hospital there.) The car gave him independent mobility; it meant he could drive somewhere if he wanted to without having to rely on someone else or ask for official transport, and without letting anyone else know where he was going.

Oppenheimer, as director, insisted that everyone should know what was going on and he held a weekly meeting, or colloquium as it was called, for all senior staff. It was usually attended by about fifty people, and progress was reviewed.

General Groves wanted work compartmentalized, with everyone knowing only what he needed to know for his work, in the interests of security. But Oppenheimer insisted on holding these colloquia, first of all because the work was so new that possible interactions between different areas could not be foreseen, and a new idea in one might unexpectedly solve a problem in another, but also for morale reasons, so that everyone should know what part his work was playing in this huge undertaking.

Fuchs learned for the first time at Los Alamos about a new kind of atomic bomb. As well as a uranium 235 bomb, they were also designing there another kind of fission bomb, made with plutonium. This was something that was first suggested in Britain by Egon Bretscher, a Swiss-born physicist who had worked in the Oxford branch of Tube Alloys, and was now here in Los Alamos.

But it was also suggested at the Berkeley laboratory in California, and there the idea was followed through. Plutonium is a man-made element produced by the fissioning of uranium atoms, and it is fissile, like uranium 235. So a nuclear reactor was built at Hanford, in Washington State, and a chemical separation plant to extract the plutonium from the uranium that had undergone fission in the reactor.

Just before Peierls and Fuchs arrived, it was found that a plutonium bomb could not be made to work in the same way that a uranium 235 Tomb was expected to: that is, by bringing two pieces together very rapidly so that they form a critical mass. Plutonium atoms fission spontaneously, and would do so even in the millionth of a second during which the two pieces are brought together, and the energy would be dissipated rather than concentrated in an explosion. From this time on, the problem of how to detonate a plutonium bomb took up more time and thought at Los Alamos than any other.

The answer turned out to be to make high explosives into a

hollow sphere so that they would explode inwards, in an 'implosion'. Plutonium would then be put inside this sphere and it would be compressed by the blast into a critical mass. This is extremely complicated, and it involves calculating microsecond reactions both in high explosives and in the fissioning of plutonium. The chemist George Kistiakowsky was-brought in from an army specialized explosives programme, and he designed eventually a series of what are called explosive lenses, which ensured that the force of the explosion was precisely the same on all parts of the sphere.

Edward Teller, the brilliant but individualistic Hungarian-born physicist, was calculating plutonium fission reactions. But he was becoming more and more absorbed with another possibility, albeit a remote one: a bomb that would work by nuclear fusion, and would be even more powerful than a fission bomb. When scientists discussed this, they called it the 'super'. It was what would later be called the thermonuclear bomb, or hydrogen bomb. Oppenheimer and Bethe urged him to concentrate on the task in hand, of building a fission bomb and winning the war, but they could not overcome his enthusiasm for the fusion idea. So Bethe let him go off and work on it, and he assigned Peierls and Fuchs to take over his work on plutonium fission.[viii]

This problem of the premature detonation, or pre-detonation, as it was called, of a plutonium device preoccupied them. So much so that once, when Fuchs telephoned a garage in Santa Fe to say that the timing of his ignition was faulty, he told the garage that it 'pre-detonated'. Peierls, who was in his office at the time and heard his end of the conversation, chided him jokingly for a lapse in security.

Kistiakowsky had a separate group working on the high explosives part of the implosion device, called the X (for 'explosives') group. They carried out tests with high explosives at a spot five miles away from the main laboratory area. Fuchs became the liaison man between the people working on the fission of plutonium atoms and the X group; he used to go over to the place where the X group was working about twice a week. He knew more than anyone else about the detailed work in both groups. He also worked on the hydrodynamics of the implosion process; that is, the behaviour of the plutonium under compression. He devised a mathematical method of calculating this that is still used today.

He was an indefatigable worker. He was usually in his office before eight in the morning, even if he had been out the night before, and he often worked there late in the evening. Even in his work, he tended to be solitary. Most people would wander into one another's offices to talk over problems. Fuchs rarely moved out of his own office, although he was quite willing to discuss things with people if they came into his.

Bethe came to regard him as one of the most valuable people in his division. Years later, when he was questioned by FBI agents, Bethe told them: 'Everyone thought of him as a quiet, industrious man who would do just about anything he could to help our project.' And he added, 'If he was a spy, he played his part to perfection.'

Fuchs also impressed Oppenheimer by working out that they were all approaching a particular problem from the wrong angle, and demonstrating this. After a while he was invited to attend meetings of the Co-ordinating Council although this was for division leaders and group leaders and Fuchs was neither.

Family ties meant a great deal to Fuchs; he wanted to visit his sister Kristel at Christmas, but there was too much work and he could not leave. However, he managed to go for a short visit in February. He also wanted to see Gold again, to give him all the exciting new information he had about the development of the bomb. Since he found it difficult to get away, he thought he would get Gold to come out West to meet him. With this in mind, he took with him a street map of Santa Fe, issued by the city's Chamber of Commerce.

When he got to his sister's house, she told him that his friend Raymond had called at her house the previous autumn, and she gave him the message that he had left. He telephoned the number he was given, and thus contacted Yakovlev.

Yakovlev went immediately to Philadelphia and asked Gold to go and see Fuchs in Cambridge. He gave Gold an envelope containing $1,500, which he said he was to offer to Fuchs, but he advised him not to press it on him if he did not want to accept it.

Gold went to Cambridge and went straight to the Heinemans' house. He was met by Kristel and then Fuchs. Kristel excused herself and went to collect the children from nursery school, and Fuchs took Gold up to the spare bedroom.

During a twenty-minute conversation, Fuchs told Gold briefly about Los Alamos and the work that was going on there. He also suggested a meeting in Santa Fe sometime later on, when Gold could get away from his job. Gold named a date in June. Fuchs then gave him the map of Santa Fe and showed him Alameda Street, a tree-lined street with benches along the banks of the river, and said he would pick him up there, in his car. But he did not have to wait until then to pass valuable information on to the Russians. He suggested that they meet in a day or two across the river in Boston, and he would give him some papers.

Gold said he had a belated Christmas present for him, a thin evening-dress-type wallet, which Fuchs accepted with thanks. Then Gold him the envelope with the $1,500 in it, and said he could have it for himself, for his services. Fuchs was puzzled, and Gold had to repeat this before he understood. Fuchs dismissed the offer brusquely, and Gold took the envelope back to Yakovlev unopened.

After Gold had gone, Fuchs sat down and wrote out in longhand what he knew about the atomic bomb project, covering eight pages, and gave it to Gold at their meeting in Boston. As a participant in the weekly colloquium, he knew about the work of every section at Los Alamos.

Years later, in a British prison, Fuchs listed the information in those pages. As he recalled it, this was, in his own words:

> Classified data dealing with the whole problem of making an atom bomb from fissionable material as I then knew the problem.
> Information as to the principle of the method of detonating an atom bomb.
> The possibility of making a plutonium bomb.
> The high spontaneous fission rate of plutonium. (It is this which causes fission to occur more quickly than in U-235.) Much of what was then known concerning implosion.
> The fact that high explosives as a type of compression was considered but had not been entirely decided upon.
> The size as to outer dimensions of the high explosive component.
> The principle of the lens system which had not at that time been finally adopted.
> The difficulties of multi-point detonation, as this was the specific problem on which I was then working.
> The comparative critical mass of plutonium as compared with uranium 235.
> The approximate amount of plutonium necessary for such a bomb.
> Some information as to the type of core.
> The current ideas as to the need for an initiator.

This must all have been of help to the Soviet scientists. They had worked out already that a new element with the atomic number 94, what the Americans were calling plutonium, would be fissile, and that it was a possible atomic bomb material (the first Soviet atomic bomb was made with plutonium). They probably did not know at this stage about the difficulty of detonating it, nor the implosion solution to this difficulty, nor about the implosion lens, nor the amount of materials that would constitute a critical mass. They were interested particularly in the implosion lens idea, and they sent back, through the intelligence service, a request for more information about this.

***

Fuchs took the train back to New Mexico and joined his friends in Los Alamos. He had satisfied his conscience in doing what he did, yet there may have been, somewhere in his unconscious, a conflict. For as soon as he got back he fell ill with his old, dry cough. He stayed in bed in his room for a few days, coughing a little but showing no other sign of illness, and looking miserable. Mrs Peierls took him hot soup. After a few days he got himself up and threw himself back into his work.

The voice of conscience that told Fuchs he must do as he did was not a warm, compassionate voice. It was not the kind that might carry a nagging reminder of an elderly person neglected, or a friend deceived, or someone suffering unhappiness that could be remedied. It was the stern voice of duty, demanding that he be a good Communist and act as political logic dictates, for the sake of a better world. Warmth, affection and human sympathy lay somewhere else in his mind. They were not allowed to get in the way.

In Fuchs's own assessment of himself, his betrayals were confined to the political sphere, and outside this he was always sincere and honest. But perhaps there was betrayal in the personal sphere also. Perhaps Fuchs, in some part of his mind, basked in the superior sense that he knew what his friends did not know, that he was doing something about the things they were only talking about.

Fuchs went out a lot at Los Alamos. People invited him to their parties, and asked him along on outings. His reticence was not offensive, and he was well-mannered, a good dancer and a good listener. Some wives took him up, ministering to the needs of this thin, shy, evidently lonely man. Women are usually readier than men to take the trouble to reach out to someone who keeps to himself. Suzanne Deutsch used to take him her home-baked cookies.

One wife who had entertained him a number of times in her home sat him down in her kitchen one day and made a frontal assault on his reserve. 'Klaus,' she said, 'here in America, when we become friends with somebody, we tell them about ourselves, our family, and where we come from, and so on. We're friends, but I hardly know anything about you. So tell me something about yourself. Who were your family? What were they like?' Fuchs told her a little about his father, and about his sister who had committed suicide, and his brother in Switzerland. He did not mention his mother, nor did he say that he had another sister living in America.

One day, Ellen Weisskopf and another scientist's wife decided to go to the movies in Santa Fe in the evening, to see an Alfred Hitchcock thriller. 'Let's ask Klaus Fuchs to come along,' she said. 'It will be someone to squeeze if it gets too frightening.' Fuchs joined them, on that occasion and on a couple of other trips to the movies when their husbands were busy, but nobody squeezed anyone. Unlike at least one other bachelor scientist, he never made a pass at anyone's wife.

A young woman who taught school at Los Alamos, Evelyn Kline, and a friend of hers asked him to go with them to see some Indian dances nearby. He took her out again, and she thought enough about it to send him a Christmas card after he left, and a letter when he failed to respond to it, but he did not answer the letter either.

Several men who were at Los Alamos, asked about Fuchs,

have said in one way or another, 'Actually, my wife saw more of Fuchs than I did. She probably knows him better than me.' Yet it did not occur to any one of them that there might be, or even might seem to be, anything improper in this. It is as if his personality was so bland and quiet that it neutered him in the eyes of others, and he was assumed not to be a part of the sexual action.

He liked children, and they usually took to him and to his quiet, kindly, undemanding manner. He would talk to them at parties, and he sometimes took both the Peierls children hiking for a day.

He became a well-liked member of the Los Alamos community, regarded as a thoroughly decent man, probably with an unhappy past that he was keeping to himself. 'He's such a nice person. What a pity he's so low key,' said Mary Argo, and this was a typical opinion.

He started to drink a lot at parties, and showily. He could go through most of a bottle of whisky or gin in an evening. He seemed proud of his control, as he was when he was climbing cliffs; only he knew how much he was controlling. The drink helped him to forget what he was doing behind the backs of these friends of his. He explained this years later, in a letter he wrote from prison:

'It surprised me when I found that I could get drunk without any fears. I thought at the time that even then I could control myself, but I don't think the explanation is correct. I think the truth is that under the influence of alcohol, the control disappeared, but not only the control but the need for it, the whole other compartment of my mind.' Evidently, when he drank he was no longer a spy, no longer giving away the secrets that the others kept, but was a loyal and upright member of the Los Alamos scientific community, and a worker in the effort in which they were all engaged together, that and nothing more.

The British Government opened a laboratory to do work on atomic fission in Montreal, jointly with the Canadian Government. This was to be kept separate from the US-British effort, and the British scientists working in America remained there.

By the early part of 1945 there was no doubt that a uranium 235 fission bomb would work, but there were still uncertainties about a plutonium bomb and the implosion technique. It was decided that there would have to be a test explosion before one could be used militarily. Preparations went ahead for the test, which was to take place, in secret, out in the desert at a place ninety miles from Los Alamos called Alamogordo. (Because some people would see the flash on the horizon, even from Las Vegas, a cover story was prepared saying that an army ammunition dump had been blown up in an accident.) Much of the work was now moving out of the theoretical stage. Uranium 235 and plutonium were arriving at Los Alamos from Oak Ridge and Hanford, and the chemists and metallurgists could experiment with it. Fuchs joined the team preparing for the Alamogordo test, which was codenamed Trinity. Versatile as always, he was assigned to calculating the blast effects of the explosion.

By now, Allied forces were overrunning Germany and the war in Europe was moving bloodily to its conclusion. The original impetus that drove many of them — the fear that Germany would build an atomic bomb first — was vanishing. Yet the pace of work at Los Alamos did not slacken, nor did the sense of urgency diminish. For one thing, men were dying every day now in the Pacific war, and the aim was to shorten this war. But also they were carried along by the sheer momentum of the project, with excitement building up as completion approached, and it did not occur to them to question whether they should continue. (There was one exception. Josef Rotblat, a Polish physicist who had done important work for Tube Alloys at Liverpool University and come over with the British scientists, decided when it was clear that the Germans were not going to have an atomic bomb that he no longer wanted to help build so destructive a weapon, and he told Chadwick, as head of the British mission, that he wanted to resign. Chadwick said he could but he asked him not to discuss his views with anyone else, so he left quietly. He went into radiation medicine, and has campaigned since for reductions in nuclear armaments.)

Once, at the Weisskopfs', when people were talking about international affairs, Peierls made a remark that was critical of something Russia was doing, and Fuchs said, 'There is another side to it.' This comment was remembered because it was so rare. Fuchs never joined in discussions about world affairs. This was not particularly noticed because he was often silent when everyone else was talking.

Several people remarked on the fact that one of America's major allies in the war, Britain, was taking part in the project but the other, the Soviet Union, was excluded. Some said that the atomic bomb should be shared with the Russians, and not sharing it was disloyalty to an ally. Niels Bohr, a founding father of atomic physics (Otto Frisch was at Bohr's institute in Copenhagen when he hit on the idea of nuclear fission), had now arrived in Los Alamos, and he was revered by physicists. He wanted to bring the Soviet Union in on the atom bomb project. He worried that keeping the secret from the Russians would sow suspicion, and he foresaw the nightmare of a competition between the former allies in building atomic bombs. With his habit of wandering about and engaging anyone in a rambling conversation about whatever was in his mind, he told others at Los Alamos about his views, as he was later to tell Roosevelt and then Churchill, to little effect.

The idea of sharing the atomic bomb with the Soviet Union was not so outlandish. A number of people in high places thought that keeping the project secret from Russia was certain to create suspicion, and would sow the seeds of future conflict. After Bohr put this view in Washington, Supreme Court

Justice Felix Frankfurter urged Roosevelt to bring the Russians in on the bomb project, and the British ambassador in Washington and former Foreign Secretary, Lord Halifax, agreed with him. Even the postwar British Foreign Secretary, Ernest Bevin, a doughty Cold War warrior, believed at one stage after the bomb was dropped that America and Britain should give Russia information about it, and some in the American administration agreed with him. After all, it was said, Russia was bound to build a bomb anyway, and keeping its secrets from her, with all the suspicion and hostility that this would engender, would save only a few years.

While everyone at Los Alamos worked on preparations for the secret tests, Fuchs was making his own preparations, for his next meeting with Gold, working alone in his room. He was going to give Soviet scientists all the help he could. He wrote a full account of the construction of both bombs. Doing this at Los Alamos was much easier than writing the details from memory in his sister's house in Cambridge, for he had papers to refer to and he could give precise figures. Besides, the design for the bomb was just about completed now, and much of what was only speculative before was certain now. He reported that the bomb would have a solid plutonium core, and also a small initiator made of polonium as a neutron source. He gave full details of the tamper, the casing that held the bomb together for a few microseconds while the chain reaction started, and even the names of the two explosives that were to be used in the implosion, although he admitted that these names meant nothing to him. He explained a method of calculating the efficiency of the bomb devised by Bethe and Feynman, and also the figure for the efficiency that they had arrived at. Finally, as an aid to the explanations, he drew a diagram of the bomb, giving the most important dimensions.

Harry Gold had difficulty getting time off from his job to make the trip west in June, but he negotiated it as part of his summer vacation. He went by train to Albuquerque and took a bus to Santa Fe. His appointment with Fuchs was at four o'clock but he arrived in the city early, and spent an hour looking round a historical museum. There, he got a street map, the same as the one that Fuchs had given him in Cambridge back in February, located Alameda Street and walked along it under the trees to the Castillo Street Bridge, which was the meeting place. Fuchs drove up at four o'clock precisely, and Gold got in the car. Fuchs drove across the river and parked in a cul-de-sac, and they talked for a while in the car.

Fuchs told him he had some papers for him, but he also told him some things that were not in the papers. He said an atomic bomb would be tested soon out in the desert, and that it would be the equivalent to 10,000 tons of TNT. He said everyone was now working flat out at Los Alamos. Gold made notes of this later, and passed the information on.

Gold had a question for Fuchs, the request from the Soviet scientists for details of the implosion lens. Fuchs shrugged off the question, and said it was answered in the papers he was giving him. He was rarely forthcoming in answering questions that were put to him in this way. They arranged another meeting. Fuchs suggested one in August. Gold said he could not get away in August, so they settled on 19 September, at six in the evening, at a different spot. As always, Fuchs gave him the envelope containing his report at the last moment, and drove off.

Gold took the bus back to Albuquerque, and spent Saturday night there. On the Sunday morning, according to a confession he made five years later, he carried out his next assignment for Yakovlev. He went to an apartment house and rang the bell of an apartment that was rented by Sergeant David Greenglass, a member of a detachment of Army Engineers stationed at Los Alamos to give technical assistance on the scientific work. Greenglass's wife Ruth lived in the apartment, and he stayed there on weekends.

Greenglass came to the door, and Gold said: 'I come from

Julius.' Then he handed him a part of the cardboard top of a processed dessert package. Greenglass went into the other room and came back with another part of a package top. The two fitted together exactly. Greenglass asked Gold to come back in the afternoon, when he would have some material ready for him. When Gold returned, Greenglass gave him an envelope which contained whatever information he had been able to garner about the work that was going on at Los Alamos, and also a sketch of an implosion lens. He had been machining parts of the lens in a metal workshop. Unlike Fuchs's diagram of the bomb, this sketch was rough and contained no figures, and no clear account of the working of the lens. In exchange, Gold gave Greenglass an envelope containing $500.

Gold's account of that meeting in Albuquerque, the matching of the boxtops and the phrase 'I come from Julius', were to be repeated and discussed and examined for authenticity all around the world. 'Julius' was Green-glass's brother-in-law, Julius Rosenberg, who was married to Ruth's sister Ethel. He owned a small machine workshop in New York and belonged to several pro-Communist organizations. When Julius and Ethel Rosenberg were put on trial for espionage, Gold's story of the meeting was confirmed by Greenglass. It was the kernel of the prosecution's case, and of the claim that the Rosenbergs were at the centre of a plot to pass atomic bomb secrets to Russia.

Fuchs had another one of his dry coughs shortly after seeing Gold in Santa Fe. Again he lay in bed for several days looking miserable, and again Mrs Peierls brought him soup.

The Trinity test took place on 17 July, shortly before dawn. Fuchs observed the test with a group of scientists twenty miles away, all of them watching through dark glasses. All those who saw it had been preparing for it for years, yet they were all astounded when it happened. The bright light, brighter than the noonday sun, which lit up the whole landscape where there had been darkness before, the giant pillar of smoke and dust billowing up and out into the now familiar mushroom-shaped cloud that seemed to dwarf the plain and the mountains around, the evidence of the almost incredible power of the explosion, all made an impact on their emotions for which their intellectual concept of the atomic bomb had not prepared them.

Something new had arrived on this planet, and they had brought it into being. Many of them were struck with new force by their own responsibility for this. Fuchs also was impressed by the test, as he told Gold later, and he must have felt a double sense of responsibility. He, too, had helped bring this new kind of weapon into being, but he was also helping to give it to another nation.

News of the successful Trinity test was sent to President Truman in the Berlin suburb of Potsdam, where he was beginning a conference with the British and Soviet leaders on postwar plans for Germany and on concluding the war against Japan.

Truman recorded in his memoirs what he told Stalin, and Stalin's reaction, and this passage has been quoted often. Truman approached Stalin after a formal session of the conference, a week after the news of the Trinity test, and, he says, 'casually mentioned to him that we had a new weapon of unusual destructive force'. Stalin said he was glad to hear it, and hoped that America would make good use of the bomb against Japan. Truman believed that Stalin had no idea what he was referring to, or of the importance of the new weapon, and Churchill, who heard the exchange, also had this impression.[ix] They did not know about the secret information that Soviet Intelligence was getting, and which evidently was passed on up to Stalin himself.

But there is another account of Stalin's reaction to Truman's remark that is less well known. This comes in the memoirs of a Russian participant in the Potsdam conference, Marshal Georgi Zhukov. He was present when Stalin told Foreign Minister Vyacheslav Molotov what Truman had said, and he recalled:

> 'They're raising the price,' said Molotov.
> Stalin laughed. 'Let them. We'll have a talk with Kurchatov today about speeding up our work,' he said.
> I realized that they were talking about the creation of an atomic bomb.[x]

At Los Alamos, now that the bomb was a reality and its destructive power had impressed itself forcibly on its creators, scientists began to discuss with new urgency what should be done with it.

Some said they should emulate their colleagues at the Chicago laboratory, and draw up a petition urging that the bomb should be demonstrated to the Japanese and not dropped on an inhabited place without warning. This was suggested to Oppenheimer, who discouraged the idea. Fuchs took no part in these discussions. In any case, events were moving more rapidly than the scientists at Los Alamos knew. Even while the count-down for the Trinity test of a plutonium bomb was going on, the components of the first uranium 235 bomb were on their way by train to San Francisco; there they were loaded aboard the cruiser USS *Indianapolis,* and taken to Tinian Island, in the central Pacific. B-29 bombers of a specially assembled Air Force bomber group had been practising for the mission on Tinian. On 6 August, three weeks and one day after the Trinity test, a uranium 235 bomb was exploded for the first time, blasting and burning and irradiating the city of Hiroshima and most of its inhabitants. Three days later, a plutonium bomb was dropped on Nagasaki.

The fact of the new weapon and its use were announced in Washington, along with an outline story of the whole project. The people of Santa Fe learned at last what had been going on at that mysterious place up on the mesa. The news was greeted with cheers at Los Alamos, and some celebratory parties. There was a banging of garbage can lids and at one stage a conga line snaked along one of the unpaved Los Alamos avenues. Some people went into Santa Fe to have a party at a restaurant there. At a few of the parties, the revelry dwindled away after a while to sober discussion.

A celebration of such an event may seem callous from the perspective of the peacetime world and, furthermore, a world which is still living in the shadow of the nuclear bomb, but it was natural at that time and place. In time of war attention is concentrated on the short-term objective of winning, and rarely on the historical perspective. The war had been going on for years and lists of American dead were growing. The invasion of Japan was the next step, and this would take a terrible toll. Japan was being bombed every day, and its main cities were being burned up. Now this one air raid looked like bringing the war to an end, and it was the result of years of intense work that these people had devoted to the task. It was their triumph.

With the end of the war, the scientists at Los Alamos, like millions of other people, started thinking about returning to their peacetime careers. Most of the seventeen British scientists were due to leave soon, so the British mission decided that they would give a farewell party for their American hosts. They planned it carefully: the wives would cook soup and turkeys for 150 people in their separate kitchens, and then rush them over to Fuller's Lodge as soon as the communal meal was over and the dining-hall vacated. For dessert they would make trifle, a dish unknown to Americans, mixing it in vats.

The high point of the evening would be the entertainment: a British pantomime, *Babes in the Wood,* with the scientists as the babes and a security officer portrayed as the wicked witch. Among the other pleasures was to be Otto Frisch's performance as an Indian maiden. Fuchs was not persuaded to play a part in the pantomime, but he volunteered to drive into Santa Fe to buy the drink for the party. He went just a few days before it was due to take place, on Tuesday, 19 September.

This time, he did not prepare papers for his Soviet recipients beforehand. Perhaps he was being more cautious, and did not want to risk anyone finding incriminating papers on him. He set out along the winding, empty road to Santa Fe, past scrublands and vistas of mesas and canyons, then pulled over to the side and wrote out his report for the Russians, sitting in his car.

He had worked out the present rate of production of uranium 235 and plutonium at the production plants at Oak Ridge and Hanford and he gave these figures — 100 kilograms a month and twenty kilograms a month respectively. This would give an idea of how many atomic bombs America could make. Since Germany and Japan were no longer the enemies, it seemed pertinent to tell the Russians this. He wrote down a few more details of the design of the two atomic bombs. He said a suggestion for a 'mixed' bomb using uranium 235 and plutonium was being considered.

Gold had flown out to Albuquerque by way of Chicago, and arrived at the rendezvous point at Bishop's Lodge Road, on the outskirts of Santa Fe, at six o'clock. Fuchs, meanwhile, bought the drink and arrived twenty minutes late, apologizing. Gold got into the car, pushing the bottles aside, and they drove up into the hills just outside Santa Fe. As darkness came and they looked down on the twinkling lights appearing among the sand-coloured adobe buildings, Fuchs talked to Gold more fully than he had ever talked to him before.

Now Gold and everyone else knew about atomic bombs. Fuchs told Gold that he was awestruck by what had happened, and he was upset at the destruction that the bombs had caused.

He said there was no longer a complete interchange of information between the Americans and British at Los Alamos. He told him that he was becoming anxious that the British authorities might locate his father and bring him to England. He was worried about his father's health, but he was worried also that his father might inadvertently give away his Communist past.

He also said he expected to return to England either at the end of the year or early the following year. He said his sister Kristel would know when he returned, and Gold could find out from her. This time, he had worked out himself a method of contacting a Soviet intelligence agent in England, and he gave Gold the instructions. The rendezvous place would be a London underground station, Mornington Crescent. His contact should wait for him there on the first Sunday of each month, at eight o'clock in the evening. He should carry a bundle of books; Fuchs himself would carry a copy of *Life* magazine.

Eventually, Fuchs gave Gold the envelope with his report, and dropped him off near the centre of town, where he could get a bus. Then he drove back to Los Alamos with the wine and spirits for the party, to find that his friends were worried about him because he had been away so long. He and Harry Gold never met again. He still did not know Gold's name.

***

Feynman suggested to Fuchs that instead of going back to England, where living conditions were difficult in the aftermath of the war, he might try to get an academic post in America. He should have no difficulty after his work in Los Alamos, he thought. But Fuchs turned down the idea. 'Britain has been good to me. I feel I owe it to Britain to work there,' he told him.

As he had betrayed Britain's secrets and planned to go on doing so, one might see duplicity in his reply, but it is more likely that he was sincere and that any irony was unconscious. He really did appreciate the way he was accepted in Britain, and he was coming to feel that he belonged with British people. His activities on the part of the Soviet Union were locked away in that other compartment of his mind, where feelings of gratitude had no place. Certainly he seems to have given no thought to doing what he was instructed by the Communist Party to do when he crossed the German border into France in 1933, and return to post-Nazi Germany to contribute his skills to the rebuilding of the country, not even to the Communist Germany that was being created in the Soviet occupation zone.

The British party for the Americans was a great success. After this most of the British returned home, but Fuchs was invited to stay a few months longer, and he accepted. Genia Peierls and Mici Teller decided that before the Peierls left they would all have a two-week holiday in Mexico City, along with Fuchs. Fuchs agreed readily, and offered his car for the trip, but Teller begged off, saying that he had too much work to do. Mici said she would come anyway. Fuchs was due to visit the Montreal laboratory so they decided to start their holiday when he returned. They arranged to meet him at Albuquerque Airport, and begin the journey from there.

He was going to Montreal to meet two British civil servants who had gone to Canada on a recruiting mission. Prime Minister Clement Attlee had announced in Parliament the previous month that Britain would have its own atomic energy programme, and said: 'A research and experimental establishment will be created covering all aspects of atomic energy.' The two civil servants were recruiting people for this establishment among the British scientists in America and Canada. The man chosen to be its director was Professor John Cockcroft (soon to be Sir John), the head of the Montreal laboratory.

On the advice of Chadwick and Cockcroft, the civil servants

offered Fuchs a senior position. He was excessively cautious about accepting, and wrote: 'Before accepting any permanent appointment, I would like to be sure that this would not prevent me from leaving the establishment in a few years if I wish to do so.' But the appointment was confirmed.

The holiday in Mexico was a happy one. Everyone was in a good frame of mind. The car's big end broke on the way there, and they had to spend two days in the small town of Marfa, Texas. Fuchs wrote to a colleague: 'We are sitting for two days in this Texas metropolis of 3,000 inhabitants whilst the car is being stripped to the bone and reborn to a new prime of life — I hope.'

After this hold-up, they decided that they would drive through the night to make up for lost time. The two men took turns driving, and the women took turns staying up to talk to the driver to ensure that he did not fall asleep at the wheel.

In Mexico City they did all the expected tourist things. Fuchs was an appreciative sightseer and seemed to enjoy it all. They sailed on flower-bedecked boats among the floating gardens of Xochimilco, they marvelled at the Basilica of Guadeloupe and at the piety of the Mexicans who made the pilgrimage there, they bribed a policeman who stopped them for a traffic offence. They disagreed over a bullfight. The Peierls wanted to go to one, Fuchs said it was cruel to the bull and the horses and he would not go, and Mici Teller supported him. So the Peierls went to a bullfight and the other two stayed behind.

Fuchs sent a toy from Mexico to his six-year-old nephew in Cambridge, Stephen Heineman. He bought a piece of silver jewellery for Suzanne Deutsch, who had given him her home-baked cookies, and when he got back to Los Alamos he presented it to her with a courtly little poem addressing her as a 'spoiler of men*. This was a farewell present before Martin and Suzanne Deutsch left; he was to take up a post at MIT. Fuchs also bought a Navajo bracelet with a large turquoise stone for Genia Peierls, and presented it to her before the Peierls left for England.

For those who remained at Los Alamos after the war there was more work to be done on atomic weapons, on making them more efficient and producing them more economically. Then preparations began for the first postwar atomic bomb test, scheduled for late 1946 at Bikini Atoll. As a Briton, Fuchs was given no part to play in these. However, when a physicist who was doing experiments for the test, Louis Slotin, was killed by a burst of radiation in a laboratory accident, Fuchs was assigned the task of working out exactly what had happened and how. There were to be echoes of this later on in his career, back in Britain, when he worked on radiation dangers.

Another big step in destructive power was now on the horizon, as great in its magnification as the jump from high explosives to the atomic bomb. This was the hydrogen bomb, called by the scientists simply the 'super', the prospect that had captivated Edward Teller. It was a bomb that would release energy by nuclear fusion, and would employ a fission bomb as a trigger. No one outside the small world of atomic physics knew about this possibility, nor could most people imagine it, reeling still from the shock of the power of the atomic bomb. It might not work, but it was a fascinating idea and now it was discussed purposefully at Los Alamos. Teller gave several talks on the subject.

Fuchs contributed a suggestion of a way to ignite a fusion explosion using the implosion technique. It turned out not to have any relevance to the way that a hydrogen bomb was actually built, but not much else that was said at this time had either. Fuchs took part in all the discussions and, by the time he left Los Alamos, he knew as much as anyone else there about the 'super'. But no one's knowledge had advanced far beyond the original concept, and no one knew how to make a hydrogen bomb work, or even for certain whether it could be done.

Meanwhile, an event took place in Ottawa, unreported at first, that set off a chain of other events that was to touch the feelings of all the scientists involved in the atomic bomb programme, and of Fuchs in particular. On 5 September 1945, three weeks after the end of the war, a twenty-six-year-old cipher clerk at the Soviet Embassy, Igor Gouzenko, walked out of his office carrying a file of 100 documents that he had stolen from a safe. These contained details of a spy network run from the Soviet Embassy. His intention was to alert the Canadian authorities, and then make a new home in Canada for himself and his wife and their baby son.

He took the documents to a newspaper and to the Prime Minister's office, and was turned away from both places. The newspaper reporter gave no credibility to this foreigner with a strange story; the Prime Minister's office refused to have any dealings with a junior clerk at the embassy of a friendly power outside normal diplomatic channels. Only when he sought refuge in a neighbour's apartment from pursuers from his embassy, and the neighbour called the police, did his story and his stolen documents come to the attention of the authorities.

Most of us have grown up in a world in which the Western powers and the Soviet Union are adversaries, in which espionage is a normal weapon in this adversarial contest, and both sides try to suborn the nationals of the other. But in 1945, in the immediate aftermath of the victory that Russia and the Western powers had won together, such ideas were remote from the minds of the public, and played a very small part in the thinking even of Western governments. Even when the Gouzenko documents were analysed and the existence of the spy ring was revealed, the Canadian Government hesitated to act for fear of damaging the prospects of co-operation between the Soviet Union and the Western powers in the postwar world.

The documents revealed that several Canadians and one Englishman were spying for Russia. The Englishman was

Alan Nunn May, a bachelor with a rather colourless but pleasant enough personality, an extremely able physicist, who worked in the Montreal laboratory of the atom bomb project. His induction into espionage two years earlier came about because the Soviet intelligence service knew by then that a major programme to build an atomic bomb was under way.

Soviet intelligence sent a message to their station in Ottawa, and presumably to other stations as well, with instructions to try to get any information they could on this programme. Nunn May had been spotted as a potential recruit already, before he went to Canada, because of his known pro-Soviet sympathies. He was approached in Canada by a Soviet agent, and agreed to help. All this was disclosed in the papers that Gouzenko gave the authorities.

Nunn May was able to give the Russians details of the work in the Montreal laboratory. He also stole from the laboratory minute samples of uranium 235 and another fissionable isotope that is created artificially, uranium 233. These were so important that a colonel on the staff of the military attaché at the Soviet Embassy flew with them to Moscow.

Nunn May returned to England soon after the end of the war and took a teaching post at King's College, London University. Arrangements were made for him to contact a Soviet agent in London. Special Branch police officers from Scotland Yard kept him under surveillance. Gouzenko's defection and the discovery of the papers were still secret. Then, on 15 February, the Canadian Prime Minister, Mackenzie King, announced that evidence of a spy ring had been uncovered, Canadian police made thirteen arrests, and Special Branch officers called on Nunn May. He confessed five days later.

The discovery of the spy ring was a shock to the Western public, and Nunn May's arrest was a shock to the atomic scientists in particular. The day after it was announced several people were discussing it at Los Alamos, including Fuchs, Egon Bretscher and his wife Hannah, and Else Placzek. She was the wife of the Czech-born scientist Ernest Placzek, but she had previously been married to a physicist working in the Montreal laboratory. She had known Nunn May in Montreal, so the others all asked her what he was like.

She found it difficult to ascribe any special characteristics to him. She said he was very quiet and one did not notice him much, and then she said, 'He was just a nice, quiet bachelor, very helpful at parties. Just like Klaus here.' Fuchs flushed and became visibly uncomfortable. The others assumed this was just because attention was drawn to him.

One of the people questioned in the follow-up to the Gouzenko disclosures was Israel Halperin, Professor of Mathematics at Queen's University, Windsor, Ontario, and a member of the Canadian Communist Party. His papers were searched and Fuchs's name was found. This was only because Halperin had been given Fuchs's name by a friend of Kristel Heineman's when Fuchs was in the internment camp in Canada, and he sent Fuchs some magazines while he was in the camp. The two had never met. None the less, this information was passed on to the British security authorities, along with many other minor details arising out of the investigations, but not until 1949. (Halperin was charged with espionage but acquitted.)

Nunn May's trial in Britain and the reaction to it provide some insights into the political atmosphere of the time, as well as bearing on Fuchs's own actions. The Attorney General, Sir Hartley Shawcross, prosecuted. Nunn May pleaded guilty to the offence, but his defence counsel, Gerald Gardiner, KC, made a strong speech in mitigation. He pointed out that the charge referred to communicating information 'which was calculated to be or might be useful to an enemy'. But, he said, when the information was passed over, the Soviet Union was a valued ally; Soviet forces were advancing on Berlin, while

British troops had not yet reached the Rhine.

At this point Sir Hartley Shawcross rose with an interjection. 'My Lord, I think I ought to make it abundantly clear that there is no kind of suggestion that the Russians are enemies or potential enemies,' he said. 'The court has already decided that the offence consists in the communication of information to unauthorized persons — it might be to Your Lordship, it might be to me, it might be to anyone.'

Gardiner also referred to a statement that Winston Churchill had made in Parliament at one point during the war that Britain was giving Russia any technical information that could be of use in the war effort. Rightly or wrongly, he said, Nunn May felt indignant that this promise was not being kept.

Nunn May was sentenced to ten years' imprisonment. A lot of people said the sentence was harsh in the circumstances. After all, he had given the information to the Russians, not to the other side. The Association of Scientific Workers asked for a reduction in the sentence. A delegation led by Harold Laski, the Chairman of the Labour Party and its principal political philosopher, called at the Home Office, also to ask for the sentence to be reduced.

There was another, lesser breach of security regulations in favour of an ally which has never been reported. At Los Alamos Edward Teller, pursuing work on a 'super', a hydrogen bomb, joined Egon Bretscher to make some calculations into deuterium — tritium reactions, which would be relevant to this. Bretscher decided that since he was there with the British group of scientists, Britain was entitled to have the results of this work, although he knew that it would be classified secret by the Los Alamos laboratory. Fuchs was going to return to England in early June, a little before the Bretschers, and he would travel by way of Washington. So Bretscher gave him a paper containing his calculations and asked him if he would take it to James Chadwick, who was still in Washington.

The day he was to go, Hannah Bretscher was out shopping and she noticed that security guards at the gate were searching every car that was leaving. The reason — although she did not appreciate this at the time — was that items of equipment had been disappearing from the laboratories. She reported this to her husband, and he suggested that she should warn Fuchs that he might be searched as he left. So she went over to Fuchs's room in the big house and told him. Fuchs shrugged off his anxieties. 'It's quite all right. I'm used to carrying secret reports,' he told her. The next moment he seemed flustered and, as if searching for something to say, he suddenly offered her a drink, although it was the early afternoon and not a normal drinking time.

Fuchs drove out of the gate without any trouble. He was accompanied by A. P. French, an American scientist who was remaining at Los Alamos; Fuchs had sold him his car on condition that he could drive it to Albuquerque Airport and hand it over there. He flew to Washington and met Chadwick, and then went to Cambridge for one more visit to the Heinemans. After this he was going to Schenectady to see Hans Bethe; he took his sister along to give her a break from the children and, since she said she had never flown before, they went by plane. (As always, he was meticulous, in submitting his expense accounts, in subtracting any extra cost involved in the side trips to Cambridge and Schenectady, since these were made for personal reasons.) Then he went on to the Montreal laboratory.

He was going to return to England by sea, but while he was with the Heinemans in Cambridge he received a cable from Cockcroft. The promised establishment was already set up, at Harwell, and it had been decided that Fuchs would be the head of the Theoretical Physics Division, one of seven division heads. Cockcroft asked him in his cable to attend a meeting of the Steering Committee on 1 July. So Fuchs flew back from

Montreal in an RAF transport plane on 27 June.

He attended the Steering Committee meeting, but did not take up his post immediately. First he went to Germany where, as well as meeting some German scientists, he had a brief reunion with his father. They had not seen each other since the young Klaus Fuchs left Kiel for Berlin in that terrible spring of 1933.

CHAPTER FOUR

Fuchs took up his post at the Atomic Energy Research Establishment, Harwell, on 1 August 1946, seven months after the Ministry of Supply formally took possession of the site. It was on the green, windswept Berkshire[xi] downs, fifty-five miles from London and eighteen miles from Oxford. It had been an RAF airfield during the war, and glider squadrons took off from there to take part in the D-Day landings. It was, and is today, one and a half miles long and a mile wide, surrounded by a wire fence and heavily policed, although most of the residential and recreational area is outside the fence. Fuchs came with the civil service grade of principal scientific officer, at a salary of £950 a year, a comfortable salary in those days, particularly for a single man.

The years at Harwell completed the transformation of Fuchs from an outsider into a member of the society in which he lived. He was no longer alienated from his surroundings. Now he had friends and not just working colleagues, a homeland and not just a country of asylum, a career and not just a job. If he was lonely now, it was because of what he was doing rather than what he was. It was the loneliness of the spy, not of the outsider. His role as a secret informant of the Soviet Union was a left-over from his earlier life, and towards the end of his time at Harwell, he was starting to abandon it.

He was among old colleagues and friends. Some of these were there when he arrived, others came soon after him. Otto Frisch came as head of the Nuclear Physics Division; a keen pianist, Frisch tried to persuade Fuchs to play the violin with him, but Fuchs protested that he was out of practice. Egon Bretscher also came from Los Alamos; he would replace Frisch as division head when Frisch moved to Cambridge University.

There were seven people from Los Alamos at Harwell.

Another old acquaintance filled in as head of the Theoretical Physics Division until Fuchs arrived, and served as his deputy afterwards. This was Oscar Buneman, who had been in the internment camp in Canada with him. He and Buneman were among the small minority of German refugees in the camp who were not Jewish. Buneman, who was to become a good friend of Fuchs at Harwell, had distributed anti-Nazi leaflets as a student in Hamburg during the early years of the Hitler regime, and spent a year in prison as a result; after this, at the urging of his anxious parents, he went to Manchester University to continue his studies and he remained in Britain. During the war, he worked on the electromagnetic separation of uranium at the Berkeley, California, branch of the atomic bomb project, and then in the Montreal laboratory. Herbert Skinner also came back from Berkeley, to be the head of the General Physics Division (there was some arbitrariness in the distinctions drawn between the work of the different divisions) and later deputy to Cockcroft. He and Fuchs had known each other slightly at Bristol University before the war. Skinner and his wife Erna were to become Fuchs's closest friends at Harwell.

A lot of people wanted to work at Harwell. The new field of atomic energy seemed to have almost unlimited possibilities. Scientists here would have greater resources for research than any university or industrial laboratory could command. The pay was at civil service rates, slightly higher than academic salaries. Scientists, and particularly those who had worked on the atomic bomb, were attracted also by the prospect of developing atomic energy to help mankind; it seemed to be the fulfilment of the alchemist's dream of turning base metal into something of incalculable value. Margaret Gowing, the official historian of the British atomic energy programme, wrote of those early days at Harwell:

'Most people remember a strong sense of idealism, which expressed itself not only in a belief in internationalism and international atomic energy control but also in a desire to do something to demonstrate the peaceful uses of atomic energy as a counter-balance to the bomb. There was a belief that a whole new world would open up before them — a medical revolution through the use of radioactive isotopes, and a new and clean source of power which would end the pall of sulphurous smoke over the cities.'[xii]

Fuchs himself wrote to his father shortly before coming to Harwell: 'I only hope that we can concentrate on the peacetime use of this tremendous force in the future.'

The work at Harwell was exciting because everything that was being done there was new. Never before had nuclear physics been an applied science. The design of an atomic reactor, the extraction from one of heat and power, the hazards of radiation and how to protect against them, the production and use of radioactive materials — all these were entirely new areas of investigation. Every scientist working there was breaking new ground. Some of the ideas going around seem today to be almost laughably primitive: for instance, people working at Harwell were given extra milk rations because it was believed that this strengthened their bones against the harmful effects of radiation.

Harwell shared with the rest of Britain a sense of optimism, a feeling that a new and better world was coming now that the long war was over. Britain alone among the nations had fought the war from the beginning and won through, and now she seemed to be following at home a policy of fair shares for all. British people on the whole were pleased with themselves. But there was little joy in the surroundings. In those immediate postwar years strict rationing was still in force, of clothes and fuel as well as food. The streets were gloomy, because street lighting was limited and shop window lighting was banned, weeds grew on the untended sites of bombed buildings, pubs were short of drink, restaurants were short of food, and homes were usually cold.

In those early days at Harwell, there were pioneer conditions to match the pioneering spirit of the scientists: muddy roads, inadequate housing and working conditions, and an occasional question mark over heating and water supply. The laboratories were set up in the RAF hangars, as was, later, the first research reactor. The chemists sometimes used milk bottles as beakers, and they used to pour their sludge down the toilets because these were the only drains that worked.

When Fuchs arrived he lived for a time at Ridgeway House, which had been the RAF officers' quarters; most scientists and their families lived there at first, because there was no other accommodation for them. Like most officers' quarters of the period, it was designed to give the residents an elevated sense of social status: ivy covered the front of the building, and inside, wooden floors, gleaming with polish, and shiny leather armchairs contributed to the country manor atmosphere. Ridgeway House is still a part of Harwell today.

After a while, rows of prefabricated houses were put up, ugly, box-like but serviceable bungalows, each with three rooms plus kitchen and bathroom, and families moved into these as they were finished — there were 200 eventually. Lawns were created early on at Harwell, and beds of flowers planted at strategic places: roses and chrysanthemums, dahlias and zinnias formed patches of gaiety in the bleakness. Rows of young trees were planted along the edge of the airstrip as a windbreak.

Harwell is within easy reach of Oxford and London, but most people did not have cars in the first years and bus services in the area were infrequent and did not run late in the evening, so life at Harwell was quite isolated. In this as in many other respects, Harwell resembled Los Alamos. There was the same close-knit community, the same intermingling of social and professional life, the same dependence on a bureaucracy for the necessities, the same strong commitment to the work and the same exciting newness about it. But there were also marked differences for those coming from Los Alamos, particularly when they looked outside the laboratories, whether one considered the landscape, comparing the close horizons and little fields around Harwell with the spectacular vistas and plunging canyons around Los Alamos, or looked at the narrow winding lanes, or 1940s ration-cramped meals. In those years, life in Britain was more limited than life in America, and young Englishmen, the kind who came to work at Harwell, had less money to spend than Americans, ate less, and wore tighter-fitting clothes of heavier material.

The lawns and flower beds at Harwell were the distinctive contribution of the director, John Cockcroft. He was keen on gardens, and he hired a landscape gardener who had been in the Royal Family's employ. Cockcroft was the physicist who, with E. T. S. Walton, split an atom artificially for the first time, in 1932, in the Cavendish laboratory in Cambridge, an achievement for which they were awarded a Nobel prize nineteen years later. At Harwell, Cockcroft lived with his family in what had been the RAF base commander's house, one of the few houses on the site.

His love of gardens was of a piece with the Englishness of his character. He was quiet-spoken, modest and retiring, and kept his thoughts and feelings to himself. He would go to great lengths to avoid conflict, like the conventional Englishman for whom the horror to be avoided at all costs is a 'scene'. Sometimes, staff members would want him to adjudicate a dispute and would be rewarded only with some delphic utterance and go away frustrated. In those early days, Cockcroft involved himself and took decisions in every area of Harwell life, from the scientific experiments to the purchase of equipment to arrangements for housing and even laundry. He inspired loyalty in his staff, and helped to create the strong group loyalty to Harwell as an institution that developed there. Fuchs, for one, looked up to him and admired him.

When Fuchs arrived at Harwell, he was still worried by the discovery of the Canadian spy ring and the arrest of Nunn May, and he decided to lie low for a while and not resume his contacts with the Soviet intelligence service. This was just as well for him. Following the Canadian revelations, the British security authorities put a number of foreign-born scientists engaged in secret work under surveillance, including Fuchs. He was watched for the first six months he was at Harwell, but nothing suspicious was observed and surveillance was withdrawn.

He soon became well known in the Harwell community, striding about the site with his head tilted slightly upwards, his hair receding from his high forehead now, pale-faced, calm, imperturbable, usually either silent or talking, in his slightly high-pitched voice, about nuclear physics and its applications. He still gave the impression of a man interested only in his work. The *AERE News,* the weekly Harwell newspaper, carried a series of clerihews about Harwell personalities. One read:

> Fuchs
> Looks
> Like an ascetic
> Theoretic.

He had the cautious person's habit of pausing before replying to a question. Sometimes, if the question was serious and the answer of some moment, he would say, 'I'll think about that and give you an answer tomorrow.'

For a while, he shared an office with Buneman and a secretary, a small room containing three desks and a blackboard. As often as not, Buneman would be carrying on a conversation with somebody and the secretary would be typing and Fuchs would be working, usually smoking a cigarette, apparently oblivious to the noise around him. Later, when new buildings were put up, the Theoretical Division had its own, Building 33, a red-brick, two-storey structure, and Fuchs had his own office there and his own secretary. He still worked hard, often going back to his office in the evening.

Others became aware also of his remarkable memory, one of the features that most impressed his juniors. Once, he went to another institute to attend a lecture on field theory. A couple of younger men who could not attend asked him two weeks later whether he could recall for them something of what was said. He sat down and went over the whole lecture, bringing in all the points in the correct order.

As the head of a division, he had administrative responsibilities and he took these seriously, looking after the interests of his division assiduously. He usually interviewed potential recruits in company with Buneman, letting Buneman do most of the talking. He was supportive of his staff.

He would back vigorously a man's request for more spacious accommodation after his wife had a baby, and argue to get one of his people promotion, or a rise in salary.

Meanwhile, Cockcroft was arguing similarly on Fuchs's behalf, in terms that say something about Fuchs's professional abilities. He wrote to Harwell's paymasters recommending him for promotion. Fuchs, he said, occupied 'a key position in the whole world of atomic energy. He is one of the few senior physicists not occupying a university chair, and he could be a strong candidate for future chairs.' Fuchs was promoted twice to higher grades during his three and a half years at Harwell, and his salary rose to £1,800 a year.

If there was a difficult mathematical problem in his department he would usually take it over himself. This was not because he wanted all the credit; he was scrupulous about giving credit where it was due. He simply thought that he was the most able person around. A few people at Harwell found him arrogant.

He came to sit on more interdepartmental committees, both scientific and administrative, than anyone else. In one of the occasional moments when his arrogance seemed extreme, he was heard to remark, I suppose you could say that I *am* Harwell.'

He was friendly to his staff, and they all felt free to wander into his office at any time with a problem. But he was not on close personal terms with most of them. He knew very little about most of his junior staff that did not concern their work.

He was not convivial. He would discuss a physics problem with one or two individuals in his office, but was never one of a bunch of men drinking coffee in the corridor and talking excitedly about a new idea. Others would leave their offices for a tea break, but he would have his secretary bring him a cup of tea and a bun at his desk. Most of the others would have their lunch in the corrugated iron Nissen hut that served as a mess hall, which they christened the Black Beetle, lining up with their trays and squeezing onto the crowded tables. Fuchs would usually eat his in the dining-room at Ridgeway House, where the meal was served by waitresses.

Ridgeway House was run by Mrs Edith Alexander, who was a Cambridge graduate and had the reputation of being an academic snob, giving preference to those with better degrees. Fuchs was always one of her favourites; he referred to her once as 'my English mother'. After a while she left Ridgeway House and opened a guest house in the nearby town of Abingdon, called Lacie's Court, mostly for Harwell scientists and visitors. Guests were given breakfast and an evening meal.

Fuchs moved to Lacie's Court, partly because, unlike many others, he had a car and could travel easily to and from work. It was a large house built in the seventeenth century, with a baronial hall, a sweeping oak staircase and a spacious garden.

Some scenes from Fuchs's life at Lacie's Court seem like snapshots of a normal, happy existence. Here is Fuchs preparing for a formal dinner, coming downstairs waving his black bow tie and complaining, 'I can't tie this bloody thing!' and getting a fellow resident to tie it for him. Here is Fuchs in the garden, throwing a ball again and again for the Alexanders' golden retriever, while Mrs Alexander sits in a deckchair shelling peas. Here is Fuchs coming downstairs on Christmas morning, looking over the Christmas tree for the present with his name on it — there is one for each of the twelve residents — and giving his own gift-wrapped presents to Mrs Alexander and her daughter, Joy, who had just come out of the WRNS.

He was invited out a lot. For one thing, there was no other single man so senior in status. As at Los Alamos, wives ministered to his needs. One recalls, 'He was a challenge to the matrons of Harwell, a man in his thirties, living alone, skinny and rather sad-looking. Maternal bosoms heaved.' Several couples would ask him in regularly for a casual supper. He would chat inconsequentially about events at Harwell, or the issues of the day, and leave early. He did not talk about politics, but left the impression by the occasional remark that he supported the Labour Government.

He was asked to most of the parties, and he went and danced and drank, for he still drank a lot on these occasions. But he never joined in the boisterous behaviour that often characterized Harwell parties, the inebriated singing, the sexual gropings. Once, some people gave a costume party, and Fuchs turned up as an archetypal civil servant, wearing a dark suit and bowler hat, and wrapped around with yards and yards of red tape.

At one party he let slip, for the only time that anyone could recall, that he had once been a Communist. It was at the home of John Scott, a senior physicist in the Theoretical Division. Scott and his wife Eleanor had become friends of his; he and

Scott were born on the same day, and one year Eleanor Scott baked a birthday cake for them both. This particular party ended for most of the guests at about midnight, but a few stalwarts carried on until dawn. Fuchs was among these, and he was still drinking whisky when Eleanor Scott brought their baby down for its early morning feed. She sat next to Fuchs on the couch and they talked while she fed the baby from a bottle. She touched on politics and something happening in the world, and she said at one point, 'I really hate Communists.' He said, 'I was a Communist once. You don't hate me, do you?' She admitted that she did not, and did not give the matter much thought after that; after all, a lot of people had been Communists when they were young.

He became very close friends with Herbert Skinner and his Romanian-born wife Erna, and he was often in their home, so often, in fact, that their teenage daughter Elaine came to resent his presence, unlike the Peierls children. He told the Skinners about his mother's suicide, something he did not tell anyone else. Because Herbert Skinner served as Cockcroft's deputy, the Skinners had one of the few proper houses that Harwell had inherited from the RAF. They furnished it in modern style with tubular furniture. Politically, Skinner was a Conservative.

Their home was a social centre at Harwell, and distinguished scientific visitors, of whom there were many, were usually entertained there. Erna was a good hostess, intelligent — she had an academic background — and charming. She had somewhat exotic features, with dark hair and sparkling brown eyes, and a Renoir figure. She was highly strung and she hated to be alone, and she rarely was, for the Skinners had a resident cook-housekeeper.

Erna was also one of those attractive, flirtatious women who need constant attention, particularly from men. Herbert Skinner seemed content with this. Unlike most women of this kind, Erna Skinner was not only a man's woman; she made good friends with other women also, and she got along with children. When a formal reception was held for senior staff, she got a hairdresser in from Oxford beforehand and invited the other wives to come to her home to have their hair done, and this was appreciated. One neighbour's child at Harwell went to the Skinners' home to play with their daughter, Elaine, and came back and told her parents delightedly how they had found a mouse in the kitchen, and Mrs Skinner had fed it bits of cheese.

When Fuchs seemed to be joining the company of men around Mrs Skinner, Mrs Peierls, who knew her well and was fond of her, upbraided her during a visit to Harwell. She said Fuchs had special qualities, and should not be treated in the frivolous way in which Erna was wont to treat men. 'If you must blow soap bubbles, don't use scented soap,' she said. This metaphor tickled Mrs Skinner, and she repeated it to her friends.

The winter of 1946-7 was memorably grim in Britain, with phenomenally cold weather aggravating severe shortages of food and fuel. The Peierls decided to take a break from its rigours with a skiing holiday in Switzerland. They invited Fuchs to join them, and he agreed. They took a villa at Sassfee. They enjoyed together everyday luxuries that were absent from Britain, as from most of Europe, such as coffee with cream in it and bread with any amount of butter.

Fuchs's brother Gerhardt lived in Davos, and he came over to Sassfee to see him. He was overweight and sickly, still suffering from tuberculosis. The two brothers had not met for nearly ten years, and they spent two days talking together. Gerhardt was still an ardent Communist. Shortly afterwards, he would go to the Soviet occupation zone of Germany; he died there two years later. After he left, Fuchs came down with one of his dry coughs. Mrs Peierls had seen this before, and she did not worry about it as much as she had in the past. But it kept him in for two days, while they were out enjoying themselves.

Apart from that, he was a good holiday companion and a good friend, as always. There was one cross-country skiing trip when the Peierls' ten-year-old son Ronald was trailing behind and complaining; his parents were unsympathetic and told him to shut up and hurry along, but Fuchs hung back with him, and was patient and encouraging. Their daughter Gaby was skiing by herself one day, singing with sheer pleasure, when she suddenly saw him smiling at her, happy because she was happy. She always remembered that moment; it seemed to show his unselfish affection for the whole family.

He was a good friend at the end of the holiday also. He and Peierls returned to their jobs after two weeks, but Mrs Peierls and the children remained for another two. The weather was bad when they came back, and they had a rough Channel crossing, arriving at Dover wretched and tired. There was Fuchs at the dockside, with his car, waiting to drive them back to Birmingham.

***

When he came back to England after that holiday, Fuchs decided to start giving information to the Russians again. Perhaps he felt that he still owed it to the cause; his conversations with Gerhardt might have acted as a spur, and the dry cough indicates that it may have been on his mind: perhaps he found that his life was lacking a certain excitement, with that hidden compartment empty.

He assumed that the arrangement made in America involving a monthly appearance of a Soviet contact at Mornington Crescent station had lapsed, so he set out to contact Jurgen Kuczynski again. But Kuczynski was back in Germany, an official in the Soviet occupation zone. Soon, the German Democratic Republic was set up in that zone, and Kuczynski became a member of the Volkskammer, the East German Parliament. Fuchs looked up another émigré member of the German Communist Party, a woman he had known before the war, who he thought had been in touch with the underground organization. She came from Sudetenland, the German-speaking part of Czechoslovakia. He went to see her, and told her he had 'lost contact', and wanted to be put in touch with whoever had taken Kuczynski's place in England. She caught his meaning, and was able to put him in touch with a Soviet intelligence agent. He was to go to a pub called the Nag's Head in Wood Green in north London, carrying a copy of the magazine *Tribune,* and look for a man carrying a red book. The other man would make some comment about a drink. Fuchs carried out these instructions, and the contact was made.

This man, who was Fuchs's contact during his next phase of espionage, was a stocky, fair-haired, well-dressed man of about thirty with a slight foreign accent that could have been Russian, who always drank beer when they met in a pub. He has never been identified. At that first meeting, he began by reprimanding Fuchs for contacting the woman, because she was known as a Communist. Then he gave instructions for further meetings in London. They were to be at one of two places: in a pub called the Spotted Horse, in Putney High Street, or outside Kew Gardens tube station. If a rendezvous was not kept, they would try to meet precisely a month later at the other location. When they met in the pub, they would not acknowledge one another, but would each have a drink and leave, and they would meet in the street outside. (Ruth Kuczynski, Fuchs's contact before he went to America, was still living in Kidlington, which is only twenty miles from Harwell, but she had already been interviewed as a suspect by MI5 so no attempt was made to put him in touch with her.)

He was told of a way of restoring contact if it were somehow broken off. He was to go to a house at 166 Kew Road, Richmond, and throw a copy of the magazine *Men Only* over the garden wall, first writing instructions for the next meeting on page ten. He was then to go to another place and make a chalk mark on the wall. Fuchs went along there once and tossed the magazine over the wall, but he did not write any message in it. It was only to see whether the communication link worked, like testing a telephone line. His contact told him at their next meeting that the magazine had been received.

As it turned out, these meetings were very infrequent.

They were arranged for about every two months but Fuchs missed a few, sometimes because he could not get to London at the appropriate time, sometimes because he was not well. Fuchs and his contact met only six times in the next two years. When they did, Fuchs would hand over written material, and the fair-haired man would go away for a few minutes and then come back; apparently he was giving the reports to someone else. At one point he suggested to Fuchs that he go to Paris to meet someone who could better deal with the technical information he was handing over. Fuchs did not go, but he remembered the name and address: Vassily Soukhomline, 2 rue Adolphe Bartholi.

Once, at Harwell, someone was chatting with Fuchs about Alan Nunn May, and he said he could not understand why Nunn May took some small sums of money from the Russians. Fuchs said he might have done so as a sign of his commitment to them. This idea stuck in his mind, and he did something he had not done before: he accepted £100 as a cash payment from his Soviet contact. This was too small a sum to be either a proper reward for his services or a real inducement to continue them. He took the money as an assurance of his commitment and his loyalty, after being out of contact for a time. For someone as independent as Fuchs, accepting the money was a gesture of humility, a bending of the knee.

He soon had an item of information to give to the Russians that was so secret that his Harwell colleagues did not know it. This was that Britain was building its own atomic bomb.

The decision was taken in January 1947 by Prime Minister Attlee and a small group of his Cabinet ministers. It was not a very controversial decision. Britain was then a world power, one of the big three that had won the war. It relied on itself for defence (NATO was two years in the future). Few people in Britain, or in America for that matter, doubted that Britain should have all the weapons that another big power had. None the less, Britain was going through a desperate time economically that winter, and there might have been criticism at the launching of this programme just then, so the decision was kept secret and not even the full cabinet was told. Work began under William (now Lord) Penney, who had been at Los Alamos for a while and was now the man in charge of all weapons research under the Ministry of Defence.

Few people at Harwell — perhaps no one — knew as much about atomic bombs as Fuchs, so he was assigned to do the theoretical work. It was decided very early on that it would be a plutonium bomb, and Fuchs's knowledge of plutonium reactions and implosion technique, acquired at Los Alamos, was very valuable. When he and a few others at Harwell who were working on the project went to see Penney at the Ministry of Defence weapons establishment at Fort Halstead, Kent, they did not tell anyone else where they were going.

Fuchs put his best effort into this work. He argued with Penney against building the kind of bomb they could build most quickly in favour of going for a more sophisticated weapon with an eye on longer-term development. When he was providing information to Russia, he did everything he could to help Russia, but on those days when he was working on the atomic bomb for Britain, he was doing his best for the British bomb.

The existence of the bomb programme was not revealed until May 1948, and then only in answer to a formal question in Parliament. A Labour Member asked whether the Minister of Defence was satisfied with progress in developing the most modern weapons. The Minister, A. V. Alexander, replied: 'Yes, sir. As was made clear in the Statement Relating to Defence, 1948, research and development continue to receive the highest priority in the defence field, and all kinds of weapons, including atomic weapons, are being developed.'[xiii]

Thanks to Fuchs, the Russians knew about the British bomb programme before some British Cabinet ministers. As the programme advanced, Fuchs gave them the figures of British plutonium production, which told them how many bombs Britain could produce, and gave them details of the plutonium reactor to be built at Windscale. He also told them some things that were left over from Los Alamos. He gave them more details of the construction of the plutonium bomb, and the problems caused by spontaneous fission in plutonium.

He made his own calculations of the power of the Hiroshima and Nagasaki bombs, and gave them the results of these. He also recounted the ideas going around Harwell for different kinds of reactors, including the fast breeder reactor, which he was particularly involved with. All this would be useful to Soviet scientists working in the area.

They were working in this area. After Hiroshima, Stalin had given orders to put the atomic bomb programme into high gear. The project became an empire, over which Igor Kurchatov ruled. Laboratories were expanded, factories to build fissionable materials were set up in sparsely inhabited areas beyond the Urals, and a new programme to explore for uranium was mounted. In later stages, uranium 235 diffusion was given less attention as the Soviet scientists decided to take the plutonium route to their first atomic bomb.

As before, Soviet scientists absorbed Fuchs's information and sent back questions. The first postwar American atomic bomb test was staged at Bikini in September 1946, and he was asked about this, although he had no direct information to give them. He was also asked about American plutonium production, which related to how many atomic bombs America had. He could give them an idea of British production but not of American.

He was asked about the 'tritium bomb', which he assumed

meant the super, for most ideas of a fusion explosive involved the use of tritium. He told them all he could about the thinking at Los Alamos before he left on how a super might work. He also gave them some relevant figures on the deuterium-tritium reactions, which may have been the same ones that he smuggled out of Los Alamos at Bretscher's request to give to Chadwick. He said later that the question about tritium showed that the Russians had another source of information at Los Alamos. But Soviet scientists could have foreseen the possibility of a super, and could have foreseen that it would work with tritium, just as American scientists did.

There was a much stronger indication that the Russians had another source of information in the British atomic energy programme. Fuchs was asked about a specific report produced at the Chalk River, Ontario, reactor, which he had never seen or heard of. He was also told that there was a report on 'mixing devices' and was asked whether he could get it. He had not seen this, but he found it at Harwell and provided the Russians with extracts.

In the summer of 1950 another Harwell scientist, Bruno Pontecorvo, a naturalized Italian, went on holiday on the Continent and disappeared, to turn up later with his family in Moscow. It transpired that he had been a Communist in the past. His defection has always been a mystery; he may have been giving information to the Russians while he was at Harwell, but security authorities never found any evidence of it.

Just as Fuchs was doing his best to build a British bomb while he was betraying its secrets to Russia, so he always showed at Harwell an extreme concern for security even while he was breaching it so significantly. He was a stickler for the rules on security (so was Nunn May).

Once, he was leaving Harwell with Egon Bretscher and they were talking about an aspect of their work. As they passed through the gate on to a deserted country road, Fuchs said, 'We'll have to stop talking about it now.'

On another occasion, he wrote to a colleague sternly: 'You may remember that last week I gave you a document on the understanding that it would be restricted to members of the Technical Committee and Sir John Anderson's committee. In the meantime, I have seen this document in other hands; no harm has been done in this instance, and I don't intend to follow it up. However, it does raise the question whether at present there is any machinery to ensure that such restrictions are observed.'

One other instance of this concern is notable. Professor R. V. Gurney, who had been a senior member of the physics department at Bristol University when Fuchs was a research assistant there, was considered at one time for a post at Harwell. Fuchs advised that there might be a security problem because Gurney and his wife held strong pro-Soviet views; they had attended meetings in Bristol, along with him, of the Society for Cultural Relations with the Soviet Union, although he did not mention this.

In fact, he was punctilious about all the rules, something others noted as a Germanic trait. While he was at Ridgeway House, the bachelors there became annoyed at the way that families who lived there were using the communal rooms, and they held a meeting in the dining-room to decide how to protest about it. It was the sort of minor issue that always arises in communal living. One person after another rose and gave his view. When Fuchs got up he was listened to attentively as the oldest and most senior bachelor. He gave a five-minute lecture on the nature of democracy as he saw it, which was not what the others were expecting, concluding that in a democracy one has to respect the decisions of those in authority.

British-American co-operation in atomic energy was all but

terminated with the passage by Congress of the McMahon Bill in July 1946. This established the Atomic Energy Commission and set up a regulatory structure for atomic energy, both civil and military, but it also forbade the transmission of any information on atomic energy to a foreign power. This virtually consigned to the wastepaper basket the agreement signed by Roosevelt and Churchill at Roosevelt's home in Hyde Park, New York, in September 1944, which promised continued co-operation in the development of atomic energy for both military and civil purposes after the war. But this agreement was secret, and members of Congress did not know about it when they debated the McMahon Bill, nor were they aware of the full extent of the British contribution to the wartime atomic bomb. A limited exchange of information on the non-military uses of atomic energy was resumed in 1948, under what was called simply a *modus vivendi.*

In the meantime, there were some loose ends left over from the wartime collaboration. One of these concerned the question of how much information should be released to the public. Immediately after the end of the war a British-American committee was set up to decide what should be declassified. Fuchs was one of the British members.

The Americans came to Britain for a declassification conference and then, in November 1947, there was another meeting in Washington, and Fuchs went over there. He took a conservative line throughout, always on the side of keeping things classified; at times the line-up among the eight scientists was seven against one. (Another participant in that conference was the First Secretary at the British Embassy in Washington who dealt with atomic energy matters, Donald Maclean. Four years later, Maclean was to flee to Moscow with Guy Burgess, another Foreign Office man. These two, along with Kim Philby of the British intelligence service, had been recruited by the KGB when they were undergraduates at Cambridge in the 1930s.)

The Washington meeting lasted three days. After it was over Fuchs took up the threads of a number of friendships he had made at Los Alamos, on what must have been a very pleasant journey for him. He went to Cornell University in upstate New York and talked physics again with Hans Bethe and Richard Feynman. In Rochester he had dinner with Robert and Ruth Marshak, in whose home at Los Alamos he had spent a number of evenings. In Schenectady, he visited the General Electric laboratories, where the possibility of atomic power was being explored, and gave a lecture to some of the staff there, and then spent an evening with the Placzeks.

He went to the Argonne National Laboratory in Chicago, a visit arranged in advance that was not to take in any classified material, because this was the post-McMahon Bill era. He had Thanksgiving Day dinner in Chicago with Edward Teller and his wife, Mici. Then he went to Cambridge, Massachusetts, to see his sister Kristel and her family. At Cambridge he also saw old Los Alamos friends who were now at MIT, Victor and Ellen Weisskopf and Martin and Suzanne Deutsch.

He came back to England with a present for Mrs Peierls. It was a book, *I Chose Freedom* by Victor Kravchenko, a Soviet official who had defected, an anti-Communist autobiography that was then high on the American best-seller list.

He returned to a welcome event. His father Emil was coming to visit him, and stay over the Christmas season.

Mrs Alexander found a room for him in Lacie's Court, and Fuchs introduced him to everyone at Harwell. Emil was proud of his son, and he showed it.

Emil, a small, tubby, rosy-cheeked man now in his seventies, was much more outgoing and talkative than his son. Unlike Klaus, Emil talked to others about his experiences in Germany and, in his case, the years of living under Nazi rule. He told Joy Alexander, when they were talking one evening: 'You learn to live with the fear of the Gestapo knocking at the door.'

Fuchs, in all his talks with his father, never broached the subject of politics. He did not tell him whether he had changed his views since he left Germany as a Communist, and Emil, recalling the family agreement in the Germany of 1932 that they would not tell each other anything about their politics, did not ask him. He thought that if Fuchs wanted to tell him how his thinking had developed, he would do so. He did not seem to be engaged in any political activity.

The Skinners invited Fuchs and his father to a New Year's Eve party, and they went. At this party, someone mentioned a newspaper story about a possible leak of information from Harwell. Fuchs, so quiet and buttoned-up, was an easy target for teasing, and Mrs Mary Buneman said in his presence, mischievously: i think it's Klaus. Why don't you stop telling secrets to the Russians, Klaus?' He smiled and just said, 'Why should I?' He must have known there was nothing serious behind the remark, but he stopped dropping in on the Bunemans after this. She and her husband noticed this and wondered if they had done anything to offend him; neither of them recalled the New Year's Eve incident.

Another incident arising out of the party worried Fuchs a little. Egon and Hannah Bretscher, who both came from Zürich, spent some time talking to Emil Fuchs in German, and they invited both the Fuchs to come to dinner; they said that talking English must be tiring for the old man and he might like to spend an evening talking German. Afterwards, they forgot about the original purpose of the invitation and asked also Harwell's Security Officer, Henry Arnold, and his wife. They had mentioned previously to Arnold that they had taken a lot of photographs at Los Alamos and Arnold said he would like to see them, and they decided that Fuchs might be interested in seeing them also.

The dinner party was not easy. Hannah Bretscher was heavily pregnant with her fourth child and was not feeling well, and Fuchs was even more silent than usual, but Emil was his normal chatty self and the Arnolds were companionable as always. At one point Emil remarked that he was going to take some basic foodstuffs with him when he went back to Germany, because there was a shortage there of most of the necessities of life. Food was still rationed in Britain but Hannah Bretscher, with three children, found that she could get more margarine than she needed. She telephoned Fuchs a couple of days later and offered to let his father have some so that he could take it back with him. Fuchs refused the offer brusquely, so that she wondered whether she had said something that offended him at the dinner party. Almost certainly, Fuchs was worried by the presence at the same dinner table of his father and a security officer; he was afraid that his father might inadvertently mention his Communist past, the same fear he had expressed to Harry Gold at their last meeting in Santa Fe.

Although Fuchs was a bachelor, his seniority entitled him to one of the prefabs on the Harwell site, and he moved into one when it became available in the spring of 1949. The address was 17 Hillside. He lived a bachelor's life. He had a cleaning woman come in several times a week, although he kept his things tidy. In those days, shopping for food did not involve much choice: one took one's ration book around the shops and bought one's weekly ration of butter, bacon, and so on. A near neighbour, Mrs Marjorie Rennie, the wife of a mathematician in his division, used to take Fuchs's ration books and do his weekly shopping for him. But he rarely cooked for himself, and usually ate dinner at Ridgeway Hall, where he ate his lunches. Once, several bachelors were discussing how to get their socks darned, for these were before the days of man-made-fibre socks, and one of them said, 'Klaus, what do you do with your socks when they get holes in them?" I wear them,' he replied.

He had an old pre-war car, but then he bought an MG sports car from Herbert Skinner, an acquisition that many of the younger bachelors envied, and that did not seem to suit his personality.

Old friends from Los Alamos often came to Harwell, because it was one of the few world centres of nuclear physics, and Fuchs would entertain them. Edward Teller came in 1949 as a member of the US Advisory Committee on Reactor Safety. Fuchs said he would like to talk to him, and asked him back to his house. But when Teller came, Fuchs looked at him and said, 'You look tired. Would you like to lie down for a while rather than talk?' Teller admitted that he was tired and accepted the offer gratefully, reflecting on Fuchs's thoughtfulness.

One visit in particular must have pleased Fuchs. Robert Oppenheimer came in September 1948, as a guest of Cockcroft. He was then the Director of the Institute for Advanced Study at Princeton, New Jersey, a haven for leading thinkers in many fields — Einstein was then its most famous resident. Oppenheimer had dinner with Fuchs at a restaurant in Abingdon, and he offered him a place at the Institute as a research fellow. Any scientist would have been gratified by such an invitation, but Fuchs declined the offer with thanks. He said, however, that in some ways he would have liked to come, because at Harwell he was so caught up in administrative work that he was falling behind in his physics.

Harwell came to have two roles. It was a major academic research centre, producing original work for publication in the whole field of atomic physics, sometimes in co-operation with universities; and it was also providing the scientific back-up for a major industrial programme to create both atomic weapons and atomic power.

Fuchs had never worked on the physics of atomic power before, but he learned about it at Harwell, and contributed some new ideas on reactors. He also worked on safety, in conjunction with a number of scientists from the Medical Research Council, and helped work out permissible, or safe, radiation levels. He sometimes used to visit the MRC in London in company with one or two others from Harwell. On a couple of occasions, when they had time to kill before catching a train back to Didcot, they asked Fuchs to join them for a drink or a visit to a film, and he turned down the invitation, but he did not tell them what he was doing instead.

When he was discussing reactor safety once with Compton Rennie, he returned to the accident at Los Alamos which killed Louis Slotin, and which he had investigated as one of his last tasks there. He told Rennie to work out as an exercise just what had happened: why there was a release of radiation, how strong it would have been, why there was no explosion.

When the Theoretical Division had a colloquium to review work, he would sit in the front row, often encouraging the speaker if it was a junior member of the division, or throwing out an occasional useful question. When he himself gave a talk it was always well attended. He was not an entertaining speaker, but his lectures were packed with information clearly presented for a professional audience.

Professionally and socially, Fuchs belonged at Harwell, as he had not belonged anywhere since he left Germany. Always sure of his ability, he was now confident of his status also.

He was sufficiently confident to hit out when he clashed with Bretscher over work. The dispute was unusual for him but not for Bretscher, a man who was much liked but who none the less generated friction, so that a lot of his friends quarrelled with him on occasions. It arose out of a project to measure the amount of radioactivity that would be put into the Irish Sea by the Windscale atomic power complex that was being built on the Cumbria coast, a subject that is controversial today — the site is now called Sellafield. The man directly in charge of the project was Henry Seligman, who worked in Bretscher's Nuclear Physics Division. Some people were sceptical about whether it was possible to get any useful answers at this early stage, so Seligman christened the project Seanuts. Fuchs was among the sceptics. When Bretscher and Seligman wanted a theoretical physicist to work with them, they approached John Scott, without going through Fuchs. Since Scott was in Fuchs's division, this was a breach of etiquette and Fuchs was annoyed.

Seanuts overlapped Fuchs's own studies on radiation and safety, and Fuchs came to feel that Bretscher was pushing through the project against the general interests of Harwell and for his own advancement, and putting pressure on Scott to produce figures. The argument escalated, to the point where Fuchs wrote Bretscher a letter of two and a half closely typed pages which sounds at times like a bureaucratic declaration of war. It contained sentences such as: I strongly deprecate your attempts to hide behind Scott.' And 'I find it very surprising that you should force yourself into a leading position in the irradiation project against evident opposition.' And 'I shall resist any attacks which are made behind my back, and any attacks which are made for the purpose of prestige or position.'

Bretscher stormed off to Cockcroft with the letter, demanding a withdrawal from Fuchs. As usual, Cockcroft declined to throw his weight into the conflict, but it was smoothed over, and Fuchs did his bit to restore peace by inviting the Bretschers to tea in the garden at Lacie's Court on a Sunday afternoon.

During all this time, he was writing his reports for his Soviet contact, and meeting him occasionally in pubs. But the gaps between these meetings became longer. Doubts about the Communist philosophy, and about what he was doing, were seeping into his mind on several levels, and they began to erode the diligence with which he was carrying out his self-imposed task on behalf of the Soviet Union.

***

Fuchs was becoming friendly with another man at Harwell, Henry Arnold, the security officer, his fellow guest at dinner that evening at the Bretschers'. Arnold took the lead in establishing the friendship. He wanted to get to know Fuchs for professional reasons. He had decided that if there was a spy at Harwell, then Fuchs would be high on the list of suspects.

This was partly because Fuchs's obvious reserve could mean that he was hiding something. It was partly also because of a simple test Arnold ran soon after he came to Harwell. He told each of the division heads that, as security officer, he would like to have a duplicate key to each division's safe. They all refused, as he expected, except Fuchs, who agreed readily. He decided that Fuchs might be too good to be true.

Arnold was unusual among security officers at such establishments in that he was popular with the scientific staff. He had not been professionally involved with security matters for most of his life. He had been a particularly adventurous fighter pilot during World War I, and then had led an unadventurous life for the next twenty years working at the Bank of England. He rejoined the RAF in World War II and served as a security officer, rising to the rank of Wing Commander. After the war he went back to the bank, but then was tapped for the Harwell job. He was a tall, thin, angular man with a jaunty walk, a ready smile and a quiet manner. He was a serious amateur cellist and the son of a concert pianist. As always among physicists, many people at Harwell were music-lovers or serious amateur musicians, and Arnold enjoyed talking about music with them. He used to drop in on people for a cup of tea or coffee and a chat, and hear the latest gossip about who was doing what. This was his way of keeping tabs on things.

At one party, when the drink was running out and what was left was not strong enough to suit some people's idea of revelry, a few of them broke into a laboratory and purloined a flask of ethyl alcohol, which they added to some elderberry wine. They did not tell Fuchs, who was at the party, because they knew he would disapprove. Arnold was there, and could see what they were doing. Someone said to him, half-jokingly, 'You won't tell on us, will you, Henry? "It's nothing to do with me,' he said, jovially. 'Theft from a laboratory is a police matter. I only get involved if you sell it to the Russians.'

Arnold decided that the most likely security risk at this time was someone motivated by an ideological belief in Communism. He had read and absorbed some of the Moral Rearmament Movement's pamphlets on ideological conflict, with their emphasis on hearts and minds, and winning people over from the enemy camp. Much later, Arnold explained his attitude to the threat of espionage by an ideologically motivated Communist: 'I decided that by friendship and trust, I had to endeavour to inspire an individual loyalty and affection, if it comes to that. If possible, I wanted to awaken the conscience — is that the right word? Yes, conscience, I think — in the minds of such persons, in contradiction to the dictates of the Communist ideology, in which there was no scope for the scruples of the individual conscience.'[xiv]

Fuchs's conscience was anything but dormant; Arnold was making the mistake that many people make, of assuming that because another person's conscience dictates a different message, it is not speaking at all. None the less, Arnold's conception of his task could have been tailor-made to fit Fuchs. For at this time the possibility was just beginning to enter Fuchs's mind that there might be a conflict between his friendships and his espionage. He was becoming vulnerable to the tug of 'individual loyalty and affection' that might pull him away from his service to the Soviet Union.

Arnold cultivated Fuchs's friendship. He and his wife invited him over to dinner a few times, and after Fuchs moved into his house on the site Arnold took to dropping in on him for a cup of coffee. He would often be at the Rennies', whose prefab was also a frequent stop on his rounds, and he would say, 'Do you happen to know whether Klaus is at home?'

Marjorie Rennie would look out of the window and say, 'Well, there's smoke coming from his chimney so I suppose he is.'

'I think I'll drop in and see how he's getting along,' he would say.

Fuchs still used to become ill with coughs, and several times when he did he stayed at the Skinners'. He would be silent and depressed, and sometimes would not eat the meals that Erna Skinner would take up to his bedroom. On one of these occasions, when he had been ill for some days, she suddenly said to him, 'I think you're perfectly all right. What's the use of lying around here?' He replied, 'Well, if you think so, I'll go to work.' And he did.

On medical advice, he went into hospital for an investigation, to see if the doctors could find some physical cause for these coughs, but they could not find any.

In the summer of 1949 he went on holiday with the Skinners, travelling by car around the South of France and Northern Italy, moving all the time. Fuchs had one of his coughs some of the time and at one point Elaine, the Skinners' daughter, dropped his bottle of cough medicine so that it broke. He made light of it, but Erna Skinner, ever protective, was furious with her daughter.

In the close, gossipy world of Harwell, the rumour started to go around that Fuchs and Erna Skinner were lovers. There was no longer the presumption about Fuchs of neutered innocence that there had been at Los Alamos, although one woman's reaction on hearing the rumour was: 'Nonsense! Klaus has got about as much sex as a kipper.'

In fact, Fuchs and Erna Skinner went away for a weekend together at least once, to a hotel in Maidenhead. Curiously, although Fuchs signed the register 'K. Fuchs and wife', they took separate rooms. If they did have an affair, it seems unlikely that Fuchs took the lead. He seemed to have suppressed his sexual feelings, and he would not relish the risk of being found out, with the pain it might cause his friend, Herbert Skinner, and the complications that might ensue. He was not adventurous in this way; he was not a spy because he enjoyed taking risks.

One evening, Fuchs and the Skinners drove to Oxford to see the film *The Third Man*. Fuchs was very impressed with this film, set in postwar Vienna, with its picture of corruption and moral ambiguity, touching the emotions at several levels, the work of director Carol Reed and author Graham Greene. He went back to the Skinners' house for a nightcap, and Erna said how much she liked the catchy zither tune that runs through the film. The next morning she got up late. She was having a bath when she heard the *Third Man* tune coming from downstairs. Fuchs had driven into Abingdon first thing in the morning and bought the record, and then come back and gone straight to the Skinners' house and put it on the record player. He was capable of charming, even *galant* gestures like this.

He could also express friendship at a deeper level. In 1949 the Peierls' fourth child was born, and they were distressed to discover, when the baby girl was a few weeks old, that she was a dwarf. Fuchs drove up to Birmingham right away, without telephoning in advance. He had little to say and nothing to do, but they felt warmth and support in his presence.

While Fuchs's professional and social life were proceeding on an even keel, a turmoil was developing inside his mind. He was having doubts about his political faith.

Russia was consolidating its grip over Eastern Europe, and it had crushed a genuine parliamentary democracy in Czechoslovakia. The Soviet purge and the Moscow show trials of the 1930s were being repeated in Prague, Budapest, Warsaw and Sofia. The repressive nature of Stalin's rule inside the Soviet Union was becoming more clear to many people in the West now that the rosy glow of gratitude for the Soviet war effort was no longer so dazzling.

Fuchs had to admit to himself that he now disapproved of some policies of the Soviet Union and the Communist Parties. The world seemed a very different place from what it was when he braved Nazi violence alongside party comrades on the streets in Kiel; indeed, the world *was* a different place, and his own world was very different indeed. He was like a man who marries too young, and finds himself in middle age trapped by the tastes and the lifestyle he adopted in his youth, which no longer suit him.

His doubts were inhibiting. He could not help the Russians as wholeheartedly as he had been doing. He started withholding information from them, no longer telling them every single thing that could be useful.

As many people do, he was reading the newspapers and giving his mental approval and disapproval, in varying degrees, to the actions of governments. But he was acting on these judgements. As he began to disapprove more and more of Soviet actions, he reduced the services he was providing for them, as a parent may reduce the flow of chocolates or other goodies to a child who behaves badly.

Fuchs's doubts were not only about world politics. He was not an outsider now but a part of the Harwell community. As a division leader and a member of several administrative committees, he was one of the people responsible for guiding its course and holding it together. This was his community now, one he felt pleased and proud to belong to. Giving away its secrets was no longer simply a blow against a political enemy; it was betrayal on a personal level.

The ties he was feeling now were not only to Harwell.

Independently of his opinion of the British system of government, and perhaps even in contradiction to it, he was coming to feel a deep affection for Britain and the British way of life, which Harwell seemed to represent quintessentially.

The country that evoked his affection, the Britain of the 1940s, was different from today's Britain, more starchy, more class-ridden, less colourful, but also characterized by a strong sense of decency and fairness, to a degree that foreigners often found remarkable and commented upon. This was manifested in unspectacular ways, such as queuing in an orderly way for buses with each person taking his turn, and a concern for fair play at sporting events, and, intangibly, in personal relations. What this means can best be shown by examples. Here are two incidents, both told by people who, like Fuchs, came to Britain from abroad, and found the incident worth recalling later.

One is told by the Hungarian writer Paul Ignotus. He was a recent arrival in Britain at the time of the German air raids on British cities in 1940. He stood at Speakers' Corner in Hyde Park one day, and watched while a Government speaker explained to the crowd how to behave if they found a German airman from a bomber that had been shot down. He said they should call the police at once, and that they should not talk to him or do anything until the authorities took charge of him, and should not even offer him a cup of tea. One woman spoke up in protest. 'That's inhuman,' she said. 'My son is in the RAF, and I know how he would suffer if he weren't given a cup of tea if the Jerries brought him down.' A few others in the crowd spoke up in her support.[xv]

The other incident was recalled by the Irish playwright Brendan Behan. He came to England at the age of sixteen, during World War II, to plant bombs for the IRA. He was arrested soon after his arrival and sent to a Borstal, a kind of prison for juvenile offenders. While he was there he fell ill, and was taken to hospital. He found himself in a ward in which all the other twenty-five patients were soldiers. He was there on Christmas Day, and some women from a local community organization came round with Christmas dinners for all the soldiers. With tight wartime rationing in force, this must have meant considerable sacrifice for the donors. When these were distributed, one of the soldiers suddenly said, 'What about Paddy here? What about his Christmas dinner?' It was explained that this organization provided dinners only for soldiers. All twenty-five then announced that they would not eat their Christmas dinners unless young Behan was given one also. There was none provided for him, so a compromise was reached: they all took a small amount of their own turkey and Christmas pudding and gave it to him.[xvi]

Fuchs recognized this characteristic of British life, and there was a strain of decency in him that responded to it. In a revealing passage in his confession, he wrote: 'Before I joined the project most of the English people with whom I had made personal contact were left-wing, and affected, to some degree or other, by the same kind of philosophy. Since coming to Harwell I have met English people of all kinds, and I have come to see in many a deep-rooted firmness which enables them to lead a decent way of life. I do not know where this springs from and I don't think they do, but it is there.'

He had grasped hold of something, but he did not know what it was. He saw that this kind of behaviour was rooted deeply, but he could not understand how, because it was not rooted in a set of precepts, such as his Marxism, or his father's Christianity. He could understand ideology; he had difficulty with feelings.

One friend gave an account of the part of the British character that both attracted Fuchs and eluded his understanding when he was talking on a radio programme about him: 'When he started working with us, he got to know people, and he got to know their way of life. He acquired respect for the principles by which people live here. They are never really explained. We don't talk much about what we believe in, and what is decent, and what one should or shouldn't do. You just have to find out, by watching people behave. Then you find that certain things are just not done.' The fact that this was said in a Central European accent makes it not less telling, but more so.

It was not only the existence of this decent way of behaving that Fuchs had to recognize, but its strength. In the Germany of his youth, simple decency, as represented by the Social Democrats, seemed to be ineffectual against the brutality of the Nazis unless it was accompanied by the iron discipline of the Communist Party. But Britain had been locked in struggle with Nazi Germany for five and a half years, and had fought on when others caved in, and had prevailed.

The barrier that separated the two compartments in Fuchs's mind was breaking down. Feelings were washing over into the part reserved for strict logic.

Now he began to go through mental agonies brought on by moral doubts. His was not the struggle of the true believer battling against the temptations of sin, but the struggle to find out what to believe in and what to regard as sinful. It was the agony of generations of Protestants striving in their own mind to distinguish truth from error, to find their way through a sea of doubt and uncertainty without the pole star provided by Catholic doctrine. Fuchs had cast aside man-made laws. He took the rightness of the Communist cause as his guiding star. Was this to prove a false one? Was he, morally, off course?

He also realized now that in giving away secrets, he was not only betraying the British and American governments, but he was also betraying Harwell and his friends there. At the same time as he doubted the rightness of what he was doing, he was coming to appreciate the high cost of doing it. He described in his confession his state of mind at this time:

> I had to face the fact that it had been possible for me in one half of my mind to be friendly with people, be close friends and at the same time to deceive them

and endanger them. I had to realize that the control mechanism warned me of danger to myself, but that it had also prevented me from realizing what I was doing to people who were close to me. I then realized that the combination of the three ideas which had made me what I was, were wrong, in fact that every single one of them was wrong, that there are certain standards of moral behaviour which are in you and that you cannot disregard. That in your actions you must be clear in your own mind whether they are right or wrong. That you must be able, before accepting somebody else's authority, to state your doubts and try to resolve them; and I found that at least I myself was made by circumstances.

This was spoken from the heart, and from pain, and, as one would expect, it was muddled. It is difficult to fathom from it just what errors or sins Fuchs was taking upon himself. It was not clear whether he was saying that his political logic was wrong, or that it was wrong to follow that political logic as far as he did; whether — to bring this down to specifics — he was wrong to believe in Communism, or only wrong to spy for it. It is not clear whether he felt it was wrong to betray his adopted country, or only wrong to betray his friends.

One can try to trace in the tangle the outlines of the three ideas he thought were wrong. He seems to be saying that one should pay attention to moral intuition — 'certain standards of moral behaviour which are in you and that you cannot disregard'. This is a concept for which there was no room in the strict political logic which had guided his actions up to that point. He also seems to be saying that he had accepted the Communist doctrine too uncritically, that he was not sufficiently sure of it now to act upon it: 'That in your actions you must be clear in your own mind whether they are right or wrong. That you must be able... to state your doubts and try to resolve them.' Finally, he seems to have been repudiating what he said was his earlier conviction that he had become a 'free man independent of the surrounding forces of society', and to have swung over to the other, self-denying extreme of saying that he was 'made by circumstances'.

When he recounted the anxieties he felt during this period he dwelt on questions of loyalty and betrayal, but he did not talk about what is central to most people's concerns when they think about Fuchs and his work: the terrible power of the atomic bomb, which, in so far as he was able, he was disposing of as he thought was right.

Yet he thought about it, and this was the only thing he wrote down at the time and kept. Long afterwards, there was found among the papers in his office, with mathematical calculations, a sheet of paper containing three statements, in his handwriting: 'Twenty kilotons[xvii] killed 100,000. One megaton would kill five million. — Megatons [the person who found the paper does not remember the figure] would kill the entire world population.'

The next time Fuchs had an appointment to meet his Soviet contact in a London pub, he fell ill with one of his dry, racking coughs and he could not go. This was not the first time. If this cough was really a price extracted by his unconscious for his betrayal, then the unconscious opposition was escalating its actions. It was moving from demonstration to rebellion, from protest to prevention.

By the time of his next appointment after that, the opposition was no longer unconscious. Because of all the doubts he had, he decided not to keep the appointment. This was a negative decision rather than a positive one. He had not yet made up his mind finally to end his espionage activities. But it seems likely that if things had been allowed to run their normal course, he would have stopped passing information to the Russians. Then no one would know that he had ever done so. He would be living in honoured retirement in England today, probably having spent the last years of his career occupying a university chair, as Cockcroft had predicted, and the recipient of a CBE.

During all this time of inner turmoil, he preserved his outward calm, so that none of his friends knew that he was going through a profound crisis, evidence of his remarkable inner strength. There was only one incident in which his calm exterior cracked open, to reveal a man under a severe strain. This was in August 1948, when he was beginning to be troubled by doubts, and was already cutting back his espionage activities for Russia. He was attending a meeting of several atomic scientists at the General Electric Company in London. He did not have his car, and when another Harwell scientist, S. M. Duke, offered him a lift back after the meeting, Fuchs accepted. As they were driving along, a hard object suddenly smashed against the windscreen, shattering it. Duke, with considerable presence of mind, knocked out the windscreen with one hand so that he could see through, and at the same time braked hard. Fuchs was thrown on to the floor.

He appeared to be terrified. Duke called the Automobile Association, and Fuchs refused to leave the car until they arrived. No one could work out what had shattered the windscreen; the AA man said it could have been a lead pellet from a boy's catapult, or a ricocheting bullet from a hunter's rifle somewhere nearby. But Fuchs seemed to think that it was a deliberate attack, although no one could have known that he would be travelling in this car, and there were no other cars nearby. Evidently, his mind was invaded now by vague fears of retribution, either for spying for Russia, or for becoming less enthusiastic about doing so.

Fuchs's father Emil came on another visit, on his way back to Germany from a Quaker Centre in Pennsylvania, and this time he brought his grandson, Klaus, with him, the son of his daughter Elizabeth, who had committed suicide. They both stayed with the Skinners. Again, Emil Fuchs was popular at Harwell during his stay. He was invited to parties and he went, and unlike his son he would join in the singing merrily. He had an air of cheerful calm. One evening at the Skinners', when everyone was rushing around getting ready for a party, he sat in the midst of the bustle typing out a lecture on the fellowship of Jesus.

His grandson Klaus was then twelve, and he showed the nervous greediness of a boy brought up in a country of deprivation. When they were asked out to tea and a plate of thin sandwiches was put in front of him, he wolfed down the lot, glancing around nervously as he did so.

It was clearly going to be difficult for Emil Fuchs, who was then seventy-five, to continue to raise his grandson. Fuchs suggested that he bring the boy to England and adopt him. He talked to the Peierls enthusiastically about the idea, which they did not discourage, and about buying clothes for the boy.

On 23 September 1949 a startling announcement came simultaneously from the White House and 10 Downing Street. It said: 'We have evidence that in recent weeks, an atomic explosion occurred in the USSR.'

In retrospect, it is obvious that the West could not be for long the sole possessors of this uniquely devastating weapon, but at the time this was a shock. As the *New York Times* said in an editorial the following day: 'We are prepared for the event intellectually, but not emotionally.' Certainly few people expected the Soviet Union to complete an atomic bomb so soon. The best estimate given to the US State Department in the spring of that year, which was not made public, was that it would be at least two years before Russia exploded an atomic bomb, and probably much more.

Harwell scientists were as surprised as everyone else. The announcement came on a Saturday, and several senior people hurried over to the Skinners' house to talk about it, including Cockcroft. Fuchs was sitting in the centre of the room, his legs crossed, as usual, his phlegmatic manner contrasting with the agitated features of most of the others. Everyone was speculating about how the Russians did it. Skinner said they must have been helped by some kind of leak of information from the West. Fuchs disagreed: he said the Russians could have found a short-cut, so that they did not have to go through all the stages that British and American scientists went through. Privately, he was as surprised as the others that the Soviet Union had achieved this so soon. He had underestimated not their scientists, but their industrial capability. But this was a thought he kept to himself, as, also, whatever thoughts he had about his own contribution to the Soviet achievement.

The following month, Emil Fuchs wrote to his son to say that he had been offered the post of Professor of Theology at the University of Leipzig, and he had accepted. This was in what was then the Soviet occupation zone, and was soon to become the German Democratic Republic. Fuchs knew that his father disapproved of many things the Communists were doing, but also that he disliked what he saw as the selfish materialism and incipient militarism of the new Germany that was already arising in the Western occupation zones. He felt that the Communists were at least trying to build a better society than that, and believed he could usefully criticize their system from inside. Much of this he told his son in letters, and most of it accorded with Fuchs's own feelings.

Fuchs did something that people often do in times of stress, and transferred his anxiety. He was worried about his own activities, but he transferred this worry to his father's. He went to Henry Arnold, the security officer and his friend, with this. There could be a security problem because his father was moving to the Soviet zone, he said. Should he resign from Harwell? Arnold mulled this over and said the question of whether or not he should resign was one for the administrative authorities. However, he said, Fuchs might think about what he would do if the Russians put pressure on him through his father. Fuchs said he did not know; he might do different things in different circumstances.

Fuchs was drawn to Arnold, as to a father confessor. It was as if, simply by having Arnold's approval as a friend, the approval of the security officer, he was being forgiven for the crimes against security that he had committed. But also, it was half-way to confessing, and there were times when he felt like telling Arnold everything.

Arnold sensed that there was an element of gameplaying in their friendship, that Fuchs was drawn towards confessing something. He had cultivated Fuchs's friendship deliberately, but he was not the kind of man who can sit back coldly and manipulate someone else's feelings. To some degree at least, the friendship was genuine on his part, although he would on occasions deny it. In a conversation years later, he struggled to explain his feeling for Fuchs. 'I can't call him a friend exactly, but I had affection for him... Well, was it affection? More than friendship, I felt sorry for him, because I knew for a long time how it had to end.'

Fuchs told Arnold he wanted to talk to him again about his father's move, but he had nothing new to say, and he asked him again whether he would have to leave Harwell. The idea was becoming fixed in his mind that he would have to leave the place he loved. This was supposedly because of his father's position, but there was also the thought somewhere in his mind that it would be in expiation of his own offences against Harwell. He told Arnold it would be easy for him to find a university post, but he did not make any move to do so.

What Fuchs did not know was that the security authorities were aware of his father's move as soon as he was, because his mail was being intercepted and read and his telephone was being tapped. He was under suspicion.

CHAPTER FIVE

The trail of suspicion that led to Fuchs began at Fort Meade, Maryland, a sprawling army camp situated roughly midway between Baltimore and Washington that was then the headquarters of the US Army Signal Corps. In the late 1940s, a special unit of the Signal Corps was operating behind a perimeter fence within the camp, in a cluster of buildings sprouting a baroque forest of aerials. This unit was intercepting messages sent by foreign governments, and decoding them. It was the predecessor of the National Security Agency, the agency for worldwide electronic eavesdropping that was established in 1952.

The Signal Corps had been intercepting messages between Soviet diplomatic missions in the United States and Moscow during World War II; the messages they intercepted were in code and they could not decipher them. But they kept them anyway, and the coded messages remained in the files, like packages waiting to be opened one day.

The means to open them came in the late 1940s with the discovery of some Soviet coding devices, which enabled cryptograph experts in America and Britain, working laboriously, to decode some Soviet messages. Decoders at Fort Meade applied these to messages that were currently being intercepted, and then to past messages in their files.[xviii]

Going through these, they found a message sent from the Soviet consulate in New York to Moscow in 1944 which, once decoded, seemed to concern atomic energy and a British scientist. It was given to the FBI, and also to the intelligence officer at the British Embassy in Washington, who passed it on to MI5.

The head of MI5's counter-espionage branch, Dick White, took it to one of the heads of the atomic energy programme, Michael Perrin (now Sir Michael), who held the title of Deputy Director, Technical Policy. Perrin was a chemist who had come over to Tube Alloys from private industry during the war. He studied the message as decoded, and told White that it seemed to him to indicate that one Klaus Fuchs had given some information to the Russians while he was working on the atomic bomb project in New York.

This was in August 1949, and from then on Fuchs was under surveillance. MI5 put a tap on his telephone and intercepted his mail. Arnold was told. Meanwhile, MI5 analysed the message further, examining its context, and traced the movements of other British scientists who were working in New York. This process eliminated other suspects and pointed more clearly to Fuchs.

Perrin told the head of the atomic energy programme, the former RAF chief, Lord Portal of Hungerford, that there was now some doubt about Fuchs's loyalty. He also told the chief civil servant at the Ministry of Supply. He told Sir John Cockcroft, and Cockcroft's response was characteristic of his anxiety to avoid unpleasantness. He held up his hand and said to Perrin, 'Don't tell me any more! Thank God I'm sailing to America on the *Queen Elizabeth* tomorrow, and I can't be got at.'

A few days after this, in the early hours of the morning of Saturday, 10 September, Perrin received a telephone call from Alec Longair, the Assistant Scientific Attaché at the British Embassy in Washington. Longair told him that a serious matter had arisen, and he was to go to the communications room at the American Embassy. 'I'm on my way,' Perrin said, and rolled out of bed and telephoned for a taxi. When he got there, he and a senior scientist from the Intelligence Service were put into contact with Longair and a number of Americans at the communications centre in the Pentagon (Longair was told that he was the first non-American ever to be admitted there). Communication was by coded telex messages that were flashed on to a screen.

The Americans said that a high-flying US Air Force detection aircraft had found traces of radioactivity in the upper atmosphere that they thought must have come from a Soviet atomic explosion. For two hours, they exchanged ideas on weather, wind patterns and levels of radioactivity. The radioactive cloud was now drifting over the North Atlantic, and the Americans wanted an RAF plane to go up and confirm the finding. Perrin said he thought there would be no difficulty about this. These exchanges, incidentally, are indicative of the British — American relationship at this time: Britain was still a world power and America's closest and most powerful ally.

It turned out that there was a slight difficulty because the following day, a Sunday, was Battle of Britain Day; RAF airfields were to be open to the public, and the RAF was getting ready to show itself off. None the less, a Halifax bomber carrying detection equipment took off from Aldergrove Airport in Belfast. The flight confirmed the American finding, and this was reported to Perrin.

Perrin went to Prime Minister Clement Attlee with the report, accompanied by the head of MI6, the overseas Intelligence Service, Sir Stewart Menzies. Attlee received the news with his usual calm. He said he would send a message immediately to the Foreign Secretary, Ernest Bevin, who was in Washington. Perrin told him they would analyse the samples of radioactivity to learn what they could about the Soviet explosion.

Then he said: 'There's something you should know. One man at Harwell would be the best person to analyse these findings, a man named Klaus Fuchs. But there's some doubt about his security position.' This was the first time that Attlee heard Fuchs's name.

He said to Menzies: 'I assume this is being checked.'

Menzies replied, 'Yes. But at the moment, we can't use the evidence that we have.'

The radioactivity-sensitive filters from the Halifax bomber were sent down to Harwell and someone else was assigned to analyse them, in secret. Ten Downing Street and the White House made their joint announcement.

Arnold, meanwhile, was still having friendly chats with Fuchs, and was wondering how he should approach him about this matter. Fuchs came to him first, with his question about his father's move to East Germany. The discovery of the intercept coincided with Fuchs's own doubts about what he was doing.

It was these doubts that had prompted Fuchs to take up his father's move with Arnold. Arguing with himself about whether he should leave Harwell as a penance for his actions, he went to Arnold to avoid having to answer the question. If Arnold said he would have to leave Harwell because his father was going to East Germany, then that would settle the matter.

He thought at times that the best thing might be to make a clean breast of it and tell Arnold everything. But he could not face doing so.

It did not occur to Fuchs that there might be more serious consequences for him than having to leave Harwell. Self-censorship carries with it the same dangers as any other kind of censorship. One of these is that it is not always possible to limit exactly what is being censored. Fuchs had divided his mind into two compartments, as he said. The significance of what he had done, the fact that he had committed a serious criminal act — this was all locked in the other compartment away from his conscious preoccupations, so that he never saw it.

For too long, he had worked out political and moral questions entirely in his own mind. He had had to satisfy his own exacting standards of behaviour, but he had forgotten that there are other standards of behaviour that also have to be satisfied, set by the law, for instance. The question of what was the right thing for him to do had become an abstract problem to be solved, a difficult problem, even a painful problem, but not one with consequences. The important thing was to get the right answer. It is as if he had been working out mathematical problems of atomic fission for years without any idea that the end product would be an atomic bomb.

Arnold decided that Fuchs should now be questioned about the suspicion, and that he himself was not the right man to do it; it should be someone from MI5. The man MI5 sent to Harwell was William Skardon, who had acquired a reputation within the service as a skilful interrogator. He had interrogated William Joyce, 'Lord Haw Haw', who had broadcast for the Nazis during the war and was executed as a traitor. Curiously, he had also, three years earlier, interviewed Ruth Kuczynski, when MI5 had a hint that she was a Soviet agent. She had refused to give anything away, and no evidence was ever found that could be used against her. MI5 had no idea at this point that she had been connected with Fuchs.

William Skardon was known to friends and colleagues as 'Jim', which puzzled strangers, but his middle name was James. He had been a London policeman and a detective on the murder squad, and was recruited into MI5 during the war. A tall, thin-faced man with a thin moustache, usually smoking a pipe, he had a mild manner and a low-key approach, but also gave the impression of a man who would not be easily fobbed off nor easily fooled.

He once said: 'My golden rule of interrogation is: never let a man get away with a lie. If he tells one, stop him, let him know that you know. If you let him tell a lie, he's stuck with it. He has to defend it, and then he'll be led further away from the truth.' He had a good detective's shrewdness about what makes other people tick. His method as an interrogator was not to sound like an accuser, but to win the subject's confidence, and become his friend, so that they seemed to be on the same side, working together to bring out the truth.

He said once that he liked to have two facts which pointed towards a man's guilt, and he did not have these in Fuchs's case. If he had these, he said, he could use his standard approach: 'It runs like this: a feeling of cooperation, a disclosure by me, in pleasant terms, that an offence has been committed, a suggestion that the subject might be responsible, and finally, a positive statement at some stage indicating the sure knowledge that I had of his guilt. But I had no personal confidence when I saw Fuchs that he was guilty.'

He had one fact that he could use: an item of information was given to the Russians in New York. He could say exactly when it was given. He believed that Fuchs was a party to it, although he was not absolutely certain even of this; he would have to pretend that he was.

Henry Arnold told Fuchs that a man from the security service wanted to see him about his father's move and its possible implications. Skardon went down to Harwell on the morning of 21 December. Arnold took him to Fuchs's office, introduced the two men and left them alone.

Skardon asked Fuchs whether he could tell him anything more that might be relevant. Fuchs talked to him about his family and his own political background, more frankly than he had talked to anyone before. No longer certain of what he should be doing, he was not suppressing his past as firmly as he had done. He told Skardon about his brother in Switzerland and his sister in America. He told him about his politics while he was at university in Germany, and told him that he had been expelled from the student Social Democrats for supporting the Communist candidate in the 1932 election. His period of student politics was much more important to Fuchs than it is for most people. It was his last overt political activity, and so the experience that provided material for his reflections on politics.

He talked about his career in Britain, and Skardon hinted at the issue of treason when Fuchs talked of becoming a British subject. Skardon asked him what his oath of allegiance meant to him. Fuchs said he regarded it as a serious matter, but felt that he still had freedom to act in accordance with his conscience if a situation arose comparable to that in Germany in 1932 — 3. Then he would feel free to act out of loyalty only to humanity.

This went on for an hour and a quarter. Skardon never took notes during an interrogation, because this created a barrier between himself and his subject. He just sat and listened to Fuchs. When Fuchs was talking about his work in New York with the uranium diffusion project, Skardon jumped in.

He asked: 'Were you not in touch with a Soviet official or a Soviet representative while you were in New York? And did you not pass on information to that person about your work?'

Fuchs must have been startled by this, but he kept his feelings hidden as usual. However, he was thrown off balance, so that after a pause, he gave a nonsensical reply, I don't think so,' he said.

At this, Skardon decided that Fuchs was probably guilty. He repeated his suggestion, saying that he was in possession of precise information. He knew, he said, that it was either Fuchs or someone so close to him, such as his assistant or his secretary, that he must have known about it.

'I don't think so,' Fuchs said again. Then: 'I don't understand. Perhaps you will tell me what the evidence is? I haven't done any such thing.'

Skardon did not say anything about the evidence. Instead,

drawing on what the security service now had in its files, he asked Fuchs whether he had ever heard of Professor Israel Halperin. Halperin was the Canadian Communist who had been put in touch with Fuchs by his sister's friend when he was in the internment camp in Canada; he was named in the Canadian spy ring inquiry. Fuchs said Halperin had sent him some magazines while he was in the internment camp but he had never met him, which was true.

At 1.30 they broke for lunch, which they ate separately. They resumed their talk at two o'clock. Again Skardon said he knew Fuchs had given some information to the Russians or allowed it to be given, and again Fuchs denied it. However, he said, if there were suspicions about him, perhaps he should resign from Harwell. Then they talked some more about his father, and broke up after another two and a half hours.

Skardon went back to London and told his MI5 superiors that he thought Fuchs had probably passed on some information. He said he had an idea that Fuchs was wrestling with a moral problem of his own, and that he should be left to think it over during the Christmas holiday. If Fuchs were handled carefully, he thought there was a good chance that he would confess voluntarily.

Fuchs drove to Birmingham to spend Christmas with the Peierls, taking with him a number of records as a present. He gave no sign that anything was bothering him.

Skardon saw him again soon after his return to Harwell, on 30 December, the day after his thirty-eighth birthday, and again two weeks later. As an interrogator, he was skilful at playing on his subject's feelings. If Fuchs needed to unburden himself, he would relieve him of his burden. He would be Fuchs's friend. And Fuchs turned to him, as he had turned to Arnold. Like Arnold, Skardon represented the authority he had been deceiving and evading, and more so, for Skardon had accused him. In a strange way, he was drawn to his accuser.

He was vulnerable now. Once, he had his belief in Communism, the answer to the problems of the world that he had arrived at by his own reasoning process, and he could hold firm to that. But he no longer had this belief, nor his old confidence in his reasoning. If he had still believed firmly in Communism, he would have been unyielding.

At both of these meetings, they talked about Fuchs's family and his background. Skardon asked for one or two more details: could he remember the address of his apartment in New York? Fuchs could not recall it exactly. They were on friendly terms now, addressing one another as 'Klaus' and 'Jim', and in those days Englishmen did not proceed to first-name terms as readily as they do today.

At both meetings, Skardon again dropped into the conversation at some point the statement that he knew Fuchs had given information to the Russians in New York, or else someone very close to him had done so. 'It was either you or your twin brother,' was the way he put it on one of those occasions. Both times Fuchs denied it again. But he did not break off the conversation, as someone else might have done.

Skardon conveyed the impression that this act of Fuchs in New York had been merely a mistake, a minor matter that had to be cleared up so that the record could be put straight. Then Fuchs could get back to work without any more interruptions. He stressed the value of Fuchs's work to Harwell. And indeed, Skardon thought it probably was a minor matter.

Skardon's suggestion was lodged firmly in Fuchs's mind. When he finally confessed, he said of this period: 'I was then confronted with the fact that there was evidence that I had given away information in New York. I was given the chance of admitting it and staying at Harwell, or of clearing out.' (This confession was dictated. The written version says 'given the chance', but it seems likely that he either said or meant to say 'given a choice'.) Evidently, he imagined that if he really confessed to everything, he could go back to work and nothing more would be done. The self-censorship mechanism was still working.

In between these meetings with Skardon, Cockcroft told Fuchs that as his father had gone to the Soviet zone — for Emil Fuchs was by now in Leipzig — it would be better if he resigned and took a university post. He said he could still do work for Harwell as a consultant. This may have pushed Fuchs further in the direction of confessing. Because he had used his father's move to East Germany as a cover for his anxieties about his own activities, the two seem to have been confused in his mind. He seemed to think that if he confessed to what he had done, there would no longer be a problem about his father.

He was so beset with anxieties during this period that he seriously considered suicide. He wondered at one point whether he had the courage to go through with it, and at another whether this would not be a cowardly escape. Yet he continued his outer life as if nothing was wrong. His self-control was remarkable. Harwell held its first open day for the Press and invited members of the public, and, as one of the senior figures, Fuchs was a host. He played the role well. He helped show visitors around the laboratories and chatted with them over tea and cakes served in one of the hangars, apparently relaxed and at his ease.

One of the visitors was Nicholas Kurd, his friend from Tube Alloys days and New York, who was now at Oxford, and he brought his wife along. She had met Fuchs before, and she said to him, 'We were sorry to hear that you've had some trouble lately.' She meant his brief stay in hospital, but he looked surprised at her remark. She referred to this again when they parted, and said, 'Now that you're over your troubles, I hope you'll come to Oxford and see us sometime.'

'I don't think I'll be doing much travelling for a while,' he said, which they did not understand.

John Scott took a post at Cambridge, and Fuchs gave a farewell party for him in his house; this was the first time he had given a party there. He was a generous host, and whisky flowed freely. The *Third Man* zither tune was played often on the record player. Looking back on that evening in the light of what they learned subsequently, some of those who attended thought they detected an extra edge, a forced note, in Fuchs's gaiety, but this was said with hindsight. A few days later, Fuchs rescued the Scotts from the chaos of moving house and took the whole family, including three children, out to lunch at a hotel.

Another move was impending which touched Fuchs closely. Herbert Skinner had decided that he was not going to succeed Cockcroft as director, and he took the chair in physics at Liverpool University.

On Sunday, 22 January, Fuchs telephoned Arnold and told him he wanted to have a private talk. They arranged to meet for lunch the following day, at a pub restaurant near Harwell. Over lunch, Fuchs talked about politics, which was rare. He said he disagreed with Communism as it was practised in the Soviet Union. Arnold noted the qualification.

Then Fuchs said he had something else to tell Skardon, and he wanted to see him again. Now, for the first time, Arnold came right out and asked him: had he passed some information to a foreign agent? Fuchs admitted that he had.

Skardon arranged to come to Fuchs's house at eleven o'clock the following morning. He found Fuchs in a state of nervous agitation, and looking haggard. He had never seen him like this before. 'You asked to see me, and here I am,' he said.

'Yes. It's rather up to me now,' said Fuchs.

But still he could not bring himself to come out and say it. His emotions were swinging about wildly, and he was not thinking clearly. He went over everything he had said before, about his youthful political activities, his family, his career. This went on for two hours. It was a cold day, and towards the end of this time the fire in the coal stove was dying. Skardon, who knew what Fuchs had told Arnold, said, 'You've told me a long story providing motives for actions, but not the actions themselves.' He suggested that Fuchs stop torturing himself and confess and have done with it. Then he might be able to help him.

Fuchs jumped up from his chair and said, I know what you want. All you want from me is a confession. You're no friend!' This was an astonishing statement. It was as if Skardon was not a member of MI5, but had been masquerading as an old friend. Evidently, Fuchs needed Skardon to be a friend and confidant so badly that he thought of him as one. Fuchs added: 'I will never be persuaded by you to talk.'

Skardon wanted a break in the mood, so he suggested that they have some lunch. A van went around Harwell with fish and chips and other snack lunches, but Fuchs said he would like to go out for lunch, and they decided to go to the Crown and Thistle, a hotel by the river in Abingdon.

They got into Fuchs's MG and he drove the six miles to Abingdon at high speed and with a reckless and dangerous disregard of other traffic. They said little over their lunch at the Crown and Thistle. Afterwards, they had coffee in the lounge, in front of a log fire.

Skardon mentioned Skinner's impending departure from Harwell, and said, 'Tell me, Klaus, if it weren't for all this nonsense, would you be in line for the job of deputy under Cockcroft?'

'Possibly,' Fuchs replied. Skardon shrugged. He gave the impression that it was a pity that this little matter was going to end Fuchs's career at Harwell and any possibility of such promotion. Suddenly, Fuchs put down his coffee cup, jumped up and said, 'Let's go back.'

This time he drove slowly, and in absolute silence. He had made up his mind. He had no defences left now. When they were inside the house, he told Skardon he had decided to confess, and said, 'What do you want to know?'

Skardon said: 'When did it start and how long has it been going on?'

'I started in 1942 and had my last meeting last year,' replied Fuchs. Skardon was surprised. He thought there had been just this one incident in New York, and maybe one or two others. But he did not betray his surprise.

'Tell me, just to give me a better picture,' he said, 'what was the most important information you passed over?'

'Perhaps the most important thing was the full design of the atom bomb.' Skardon was really jolted. Clearly the security services had no idea of how serious this was.

Now that Fuchs had let down the barrier, he poured out the details. He talked rapidly for an hour. He told Skardon about meetings with Soviet agents over the six years, in Britain and America. He told him about meeting the agent he knew only as Raymond in his sister's house in Cambridge, Massachusetts, and stressed that his sister was not involved.

He said he knew he was taking his life in his hands, but he had learned to do that long ago in Germany. He went on to say that he had changed his beliefs, and accordingly had reduced the amount of information he gave to the Russians. He still believed in Communism of a kind, he said, but was opposed to Communism as it was practised in the Soviet Union. He had decided that the only place for him to live now was England. He was worried about what his friends would think of what he had done, and he was worried most of all about what Henry Arnold would think, for Arnold was the security officer as well as a good friend and he had deceived him. He did not realize that Arnold had suspected him, and had him under surveillance, and that he was the one who had been deceived.

When this flow stopped they agreed that they were tired and that it would be better to continue this discussion another time. They both behaved as if they were dealing with a minor administrative issue. Fuchs looked in his diary and said that he had a committee meeting the following day, so they agreed to meet on the day after that, a Thursday.

Fuchs was calm and relaxed now. The uncertainties and anxieties that had tormented him over the past months were ended. He had found the right answer. So far as he was concerned, he was doing what the authorities wanted him to do, and confessing to everything he had done. Now there was no reason why he should leave Harwell, and he wanted to get back to work.

Skardon told MI5 the whole incredible story. They still needed a signed confession from Fuchs before they could arrest him. Fuchs, said Skardon, was in a trance; he had no idea of the likely consequences of what he had done. He wanted to keep him in this trance state a little longer. If Fuchs suddenly perceived his real position, he might be shocked into doing something drastic, like flight, or suicide.

Fuchs, meanwhile, took his courage in his hands and went to see Arnold, and confessed to him what he had done. He apologized for keeping things secret from him despite their close friendship. He told Arnold all about his confession to Skardon the day before. He told him something else that was worrying him: the Anglo-American declassification committee was to meet again soon, and he was due to attend. If he were not there it would look suspicious, and bad for Harwell. Arnold suggested that he tell Skardon about this the following day. He also did not try to break what Skardon called Fuchs's trance state.

When Fuchs met Skardon on the Thursday, he said he wanted to get things cleared up as quickly as possible. Skardon said he must make a written confession. He said Fuchs could either write it himself, or dictate it to a secretary, or else dictate it to him. So they arranged that Fuchs would come up to London the following day and come to the War Office, at the top of Whitehall.

The following day he took a train from Didcot to London, a journey of about an hour. He was watched all the way by MI5 personnel, although he did not know this. Skardon met him at Paddington Station and drove him to the War Office. They went to the office that had been given to them, and Skardon took out a pen and a pad of notepaper. The procedure, like all the procedures so far, seems almost casual.

Fuchs's excellent memory served him in good stead. He had worked out overnight what he intended to say, and now it all came out in the right order. He started dictating to Skardon:

'I am Deputy Chief Scientific Officer (acting rank) at Atomic Energy Research Establishment, Harwell. I was born in Rüsselsheim on the 29th December, 1911. My father was a parson and I had a very happy childhood...'

His statement was 4,000 words long. All the important things that he had bottled up for years came out in it: his views on politics, his feelings about what he was doing, his motivations. It is an unusual confession in that it says very little about the offence. Fuchs did not go into details of his contacts with Soviet agents — places, dates, descriptions. Still less did he go into details about the information he gave them. He explained *why* he acted as he did, the reasoning process behind it, and then the doubts and conflicts that arose in his mind. He devoted more time to the political activities as a student in Germany that were so important to him than he did to his six years as a spy. Most of this is summed up in one sentence, after describing how he first contacted the Soviet intelligence network: 'Since that time I have had continuous contact with persons who were completely unknown to me, except that I knew that they would hand whatever information I gave them to the Russian authorities.'

He told how he had divided his mind into two compartments, so that he could be a good and honest friend in one while his activities as a spy for the Soviet Union were locked away in the other; this is where he used the phrase 'controlled schizophrenia'. Then he talked about his doubts, his feelings about Harwell, and his feelings over the past weeks.

The confession drew near to its end on a note of repentance:

I know that all I can do now is to try and repair the damage I have done. The first thing is to make sure that Harwell will suffer as little as possible and that I have to save for my friends as much as possible of that part that was good in my relations with them. This thought is at present uppermost in my mind, and I find it difficult to concentrate on any other points. However, I realize that I will have to state the extent of the information that I have given, and that I shall have to help as far as my conscience allows me in stopping other people who are still doing what I have done.

He then indicated how far his conscience might not allow him to stop other people doing what he had done: 'There are people whom I know by sight whom I trusted with my life and who trusted me with theirs, and I do not know that I shall be able to do anything that might in the end give them away.'

When all this was written down, Skardon gave it to Fuchs to read. Fuchs read the statement through and made two or three minor alterations, and then added a sentence: 'I have read this statement and to the best of my knowledge it is true,' and signed it.

But more was needed. Fuchs himself had said in his confession that he would have to spell out what information he had given to the Russians, so Skardon said he had better tell him.

i can't,' said Fuchs.

'Why not?' asked Skardon.

'Because you're not security cleared,' said Fuchs. Skardon was jolted once again. Fuchs was still being a stickler for the rules.

Skardon asked Fuchs who he would be willing to tell, and they settled on Michael Perrin. Fuchs said he wanted a rest over the weekend to get his thoughts clear. But he added that he was anxious about his future and wanted to get this matter cleared up as quickly as possible.

MI5 could have called in the police to arrest him at this point, but as a free man he was co-operating fully, and there was no knowing what the shock of arrest might do to him. He still had no inkling of the position he was in.

Besides, in making an arrest of this importance, the Government would have to be brought into the picture.

So Fuchs left the War Office and went back to Harwell, where no one knew anything about his confession. It was arranged before he left that he would come back the following Monday and tell Perrin what it was that he had told the Russians.

He came up the following Monday by train, and again Skardon met him at Paddington Station and drove him to the War Office. This time Perrin was there, with his pen and pad of notepaper, ready to take everything down in longhand.

There was so much to go over that they decided to divide it into four periods. These were headed: 1942 to December 1943; New York, from December 1943 to August 1944; Los Alamos, from August 1944 to the summer of 1946; and Harwell, the summer of 1946 to the spring of 1949.

Fuchs talked and Perrin wrote, prompting him with questions as they went along. Fuchs would search his memory for the answers. Skardon interjected an occasional friendly remark, but said little else.

They began at 10.30 in the morning. They broke off for lunch and went to a pub on the opposite side of Whitehall, and had beer and sandwiches sitting at a counter, among the lunchtime crowd. Most of the episodes in Fuchs's long journey to surrender and confession took place in mundane settings. They talked small talk. Perrin found it difficult to join in because his head was swimming with what he had been taking down all morning. He had read Fuchs's confession to Skardon and thought he knew the worst, but he was appalled at the amount of detailed information Fuchs had given the Russians.

They went back to the War Office and continued. Fuchs agreed with Perrin's suggestion that the most important information he gave the Russians came from Los Alamos. When he was talking about his meetings with Raymond in Santa Fe, he said at one point: 'They asked me what I knew about the tritium bomb, the super. I was very surprised because I hadn't told them anything about it.'

Perrin said: 'Let me get this clear. *They* asked *you* what you knew?'

Fuchs: 'Yes... I hadn't told them anything about it. I was surprised.'

'Did you tell them anything?'

'I gave them some simple information. I couldn't explain it to Raymond because he wouldn't understand a thing. All I could give them was something on paper.'

They finished at four o'clock and, so far as Fuchs was concerned, that was that. He went back to Harwell and left Perrin to stay and write up his notes, as a third-person summary of what Fuchs had said. It began: 'First period. From 1942 to December 1943. Fuchs told me that his first contact was in early 1942. By this time, he had joined Professor Peierls's team at Birmingham University...'

Later, Fuchs would add more details, but this made it clear to anyone with even a nodding acquaintance with the atomic bomb project that what he had done was of enormous importance. For instance, concerning his second report to Raymond in Santa Fe: 'This second report fully described the plutonium bomb which had, by this time, been designed and was to be tested at "Trinity". He provided a sketch of the bomb and its components and gave all the important dimensions. He reported that the bomb would have a solid plutonium core, and described the initiator, which, he said, would contain about fifty curies of plutonium...'

At the end of his summary of what Fuchs had said, Perrin added a paragraph: 'I formed the impression that throughout the interview, Fuchs was genuinely trying to remember and report all the information that he had given to the Russian agents with whom he had been in contact, and that he was not withholding anything. He seemed, on the contrary, to be trying his best to help me to evaluate the present position of atomic energy work in Russia in the light of the information that he had, and had not, passed on to them.'

By now Attlee, and the Attorney-General, Sir Hartley Shawcross, had been informed of Fuchs's confession. Shawcross asked for a full account of what Fuchs had done, so Perrin sent him his report. It reached him in Liverpool, where he was on the political campaign trail, for a General Election was now in progress. Perrin did not keep a copy.

Meanwhile, world events thrust nuclear weapons, which had never been far from the thoughts and fears of the world's public since the Cold War began, into the forefront again. After the revelation the previous September that Russia possessed the atomic bomb, a small number of people in America, with Edward Teller prominent among them, began to press in secret for a programme to move on to a yet higher level of destructiveness, and try to develop for the United States a hydrogen bomb. This was the 'super' that had been discussed at Los Alamos during Fuchs's last months there. The concept was still unknown to most people. A secret debate took place over three months among a small number of people who did know of the possibility — it was no more than that; the pro-super group won. On 31 January President Truman announced that he had directed the Atomic Energy Commission to work towards the development of a hydrogen bomb.

Otto Frisch, who had started the British bomb project along with Peierls and had followed it through at Los Alamos, was now a Professor of Physics at Cambridge University and no longer had anything to do with weapons. He had given a number of radio talks on the BBC explaining atomic physics for the layman. After Truman's announcement, the BBC telephoned Frisch and asked him whether he could give a talk explaining the principles of the hydrogen bomb, to be broadcast later that week. Frisch agreed. Then it occurred to him that he ought to have someone check the script in case he unwittingly committed a breach of security. He telephoned Fuchs at Harwell and asked him whether he would go over the script for security purposes. Fuchs apologized and said he was very busy at the moment. He suggested that he ask Perrin. So Frisch telephoned Perrin, who agreed to do so.

Shawcross decided that Fuchs should be arrested. He interrupted his election campaigning and returned to London to consult Scotland Yard. The American Government was told as well, because American secrets had also been given away.

The man chosen to arrest Fuchs was the head of Scotland Yard's Special Branch, the section dealing with subversive activities, Commander Leonard Burt. He conferred with

Perrin. They decided that it would be disturbing for Harwell staff if he were arrested there. Burt said, 'Would you be prepared to ask him to come to your office in Shell-Mex House and not tell him why? Then I can charge him there.'

Perrin said he would, but he did not want to be present when Fuchs was arrested. After all, they had been colleagues and, so far as Fuchs was concerned, they were still colleagues. They decided on a plan. Perrin's office had two doors; one led to the anteroom, where his secretary sat, and the other led out into the corridor. Perrin and Burt would wait for Fuchs together, but when Fuchs arrived in the anteroom Perrin would go out by the other door, leaving Burt alone to arrest him.

So the following morning, Thursday, 2 February, Perrin telephoned Fuchs at Harwell and asked him whether he would come up to his office that afternoon. Fuchs agreed. He said he would take a train from Didcot that arrived at Paddington Station at about 2.30 in the afternoon, and should be at Shell-Mex House in the Strand a quarter of an hour or so after that. Burt arranged with Perrin to be there at 2.30.

But Burt did not arrive on time. Perrin did not know it, but he was held up because the Fuchs case had already become an international issue. The Foreign Office wanted the US Government to agree to the precise wording of the charge before Fuchs was arrested, and American approval had not yet come through.

Burt was still not there when Perrin's secretary told him that Fuchs had arrived and was in the anteroom. Perrin was embarrassed, and he told her to say he was delayed at a meeting, and to ask Fuchs to wait. Burt arrived at 3.20. Then Perrin told his secretary on the telephone to ask Fuchs to come in. He slipped out into the corridor, and went into the anteroom as Fuchs left it.

Fuchs had been waiting patiently in the anteroom. He walked into Perrin's office and found a stranger there. The stranger

164

introduced himself as Commander Burt, a police officer. He told Fuchs that he was being charged with communicating information that might be useful to an enemy in violation of the Official Secrets Act on two separate occasions, and was under arrest.

Now the reality that had been outside Fuchs's field of vision all along burst upon him. He turned pale, and slumped down in Perrin's chair. After a while, he asked whether he could see Perrin.

Burt went to the door leading to the anteroom and told Perrin, 'Dr Fuchs would like you to come in and see him.'

Perrin found an ashen-faced Fuchs sitting at his desk.

Fuchs looked up at him and said, 'You realize what this will mean to Harwell?'

***

Fuchs was taken to Bow Street Police Station and spent the night in the cells. The next morning, as required by law, he was brought before a magistrate, Sir Laurence Dunne, at Bow Street Court. Commander Burt testified that he had arrested Fuchs the day before, and stated the charges. Dunne asked Fuchs, as he customarily asked a prisoner: 'Is there anything you want me to do for you in the way of legal representation?' If a prisoner cannot afford to hire a lawyer, he is entitled to a court-appointed defence counsel. Fuchs answered, I don't know anybody.'

A senior crown prosecutor, Christmas Humphreys, had already been appointed to prosecute Fuchs. He was present, and he assured Sir Laurence that Fuchs earned a substantial salary and could afford to pay for legal representation. Sir Laurence remanded Fuchs in custody for a week, and he was taken to Brixton Prison to await trial.

At about the time that Fuchs appeared in court, Perrin was

going over Otto Frisch's radio script with him, in the office at Shell-Mex House where Fuchs had been arrested the day before. Perrin altered two words because their use would have constituted a minor technical breach of security. He did not tell Frisch that he was dealing with a gaping wide hole in security, and that it had been knocked through by a friend of his.

From Shell-Mex House, Frisch went off to the BBC to record his talk, which was to be broadcast that evening. He had arranged to meet his fiancée, Ursula Blau, in the lobby afterwards for lunch. She told him that she had just heard on the lunchtime news on the radio that his friend Klaus Fuchs had been arrested for spying. Frisch said that was absurd, that if Fuchs was arrested it must have been for something minor, like a driving offence. She said she was sure the radio had said something about spying. They went outside and he saw a headline in the afternoon newspaper: 'Atom Scientist Arrested'.

Now that Fuchs had appeared in court, the news was out. Everyone who knew him was dumbfounded. Reporters went down to Harwell, and talked to anybody they could find, asking about Fuchs. Many people there learned of his arrest for the first time in this way. A reporter knocked at the Rennies' door, a few houses away from Fuchs, and told Marjorie Rennie. 'I don't believe you,' she said. 'Then listen to the news on your radio,' he replied.

Fuchs's close friends reacted as if they were members of the same family. Peierls learned the news from an *Evening Standard* reporter who telephoned him. With a scientist's instinct for getting the facts right first, he declined to comment but asked the reporter to read out the full report to him, which the reporter did. Then he told Genia. They were both bewildered. They speculated that Fuchs might have had some kind of mental breakdown and exaggerated the importance of a security slip he had made. Peierls noted that Fuchs had said in court that he did not know a lawyer, and said they must at least make sure that he had one to represent him. They decided that he should go and see Fuchs in prison immediately.

The Skinners were house-hunting in Liverpool. They were using an office in the university as a base and they separated at one point, and Erna got back to the office first. A secretary told her there was a message for her husband to telephone Peierls in Birmingham urgently. Since it was urgent she telephoned herself, and said, 'Rudi, what's all this about?' He said, 'My God, haven't you heard? Klaus has been arrested.' Both the Skinners took the midnight train back.

At Harwell, Cockcroft asked Skinner to say a few words to Fuchs's staff in the Theoretical Division. Skinner called them together. He was near to tears when he addressed them, and clearly still shocked. He reminded them of how much Fuchs had done to build up the division, and how much its work meant to them. He admitted that he did not understand what had happened, and stressed that Fuchs had only been charged, and had yet to come to trial.

The American Physical Society, the professional society of physicists, was holding its annual meeting in New York, and the news was received there with astonishment. People who had known Fuchs at Los Alamos sought out one another to discuss it. Teller, who had pondered often on Fuchs's taciturnity, said, 'So that's what it was!' Always ready to ascribe malign motives to the Russians, he told people that he believed that they had deliberately betrayed Fuchs in order to throw a wrench into US — British co-operation in atomic energy.

Martin and Suzanne Deutsch had a similar reaction to Teller's. They had decided long ago that Fuchs's reserve concealed something, that he was holding something back. They were amazed to find out what it was.

Four Los Alamos wives who accompanied their scientist husbands to New York were having a reunion lunch at the

Museum of Modern Art, Ellen Weisskopf and Else Placzek among them. All four had known Fuchs; these two had known him well. One of them arrived late with an afternoon newspaper carrying the news of Fuchs's arrest in a banner headline. They were all aghast. 'I'd have given my right arm for Fuchs,' said Else Placzek. They speculated that Fuchs might yet be found innocent, that there might be some other explanation.

Edward Corson, Fuchs's friend from Edinburgh University days and New York, wrote immediately to Cockcroft asking what help he could give, and he cabled Fuchs: 'Naturally do not believe accusations. Stop. If I can be of any service call on me.' Fuchs cabled back: 'Thank you. Stop. There is nothing you can do. The evidence will change your mind.'

Peierls went to London and telephoned Scotland Yard to ask if he might visit Fuchs in Brixton Prison. Actually, as a remand prisoner, Fuchs was entitled to receive visitors at any time, but Peierls did not know this. Commander Burt asked Peierls if he would come and see him first.

In his office, he told Peierls that Fuchs had already confessed. He said that he had so far refused to name anyone who was engaged in these activities with him, and asked Peierls to try to persuade him to do so, as a good friend. Peierls said he was amazed. He said he knew that Fuchs had been left-wing when he was young, as many people had been, but he did not think it went beyond that. Burt said understandingly that his own son was left-wing.

When Peierls went to Brixton that afternoon, Fuchs told him that he had indeed been passing secrets to the Russians, because he believed in Communism. But, he said, over the years he had come to appreciate the values of the British way of life, and had realized that he had been wrong to do what he did.

Peierls said he was surprised that Fuchs would have

swallowed Communist orthodoxy. 'You must remember what I went through as a young man in Germany,' Fuchs told him. He also said that 'when I have helped the Russians take over everything,' as he put it, he would tell the Soviet leaders what was wrong with the Soviet system. Peierls reflected that with this, the arrogance that he had occasionally noticed in Fuchs came near to megalomania.

Then Peierls told him that he should tell the police who his contacts were. He said a schoolboy code of not sneaking on others was not appropriate here. He pointed out that if he did not name his contacts, then everyone who worked with him would be under suspicion, particularly, perhaps, foreign-born scientists.[xix] And if this were true in Britain, it would be still more true in America, where illiberal and sometimes hysterical anti-Communism was emerging, with many intellectuals being accused on flimsy evidence of having Communist sympathies, which was held to be tantamount to treason. Fuchs's only comment on this was that he did not want to appear to be currying favour in order to get a lighter sentence.

Erna Skinner went to visit him, and was upset at seeing him in prison. 'Where are you sleeping?' she asked. 'What are you getting to eat? What's it like?'

'It's not bad,' he replied. 'Old — [naming a mutual acquaintance who had luxurious tastes] would have died a thousand deaths. But it's not bad.'

During those weeks in Brixton Prison, Fuchs had an air of calm and well-being that others noticed. He was at peace with himself as he had not been for a long time. His feelings were no longer in conflict with the life he was leading, and he could allow them to emerge, and accept them. He had adopted a rigid emotional posture when he left Germany as a young man, and now he could abandon it. He had to pay a price, but this was a price to be extracted by the law for what he had done, not a price to be paid by his conscience.

If he died, he would die a whole man. For in his own mind he faced the death penalty. Although he never mentioned this to anyone, it can hardly have been absent from his mind during these weeks. Actually, he could not have been sentenced to death; he was not charged with treason, which could be a capital offence, but with breaches of the Official Secrets Act. But he did not seem to realize this.

Peierls came away from the visit badly shaken by Fuchs's revelations. He had given up smoking, but in the next few weeks he started again. To Genia, the revelation that Fuchs had been giving secrets to the Russians since the days when he worked with her husband in Birmingham and lived in their house was painfully wounding. She recalled that growing up in Stalin's Russia, she had not trusted anyone except her mother and father and sister. During the years since she left Russia, she had learned to trust people.

She sat down and wrote a letter to Fuchs that was heartfelt and reflected hurt. She was literally crying with emotion when she wrote it, so that her tears fell on the paper and dampened it, and Peierls typed out a fresh copy for her to send.

She said in the letter that if he had intended to be a spy, he could have kept himself apart from other people. He did not have to become such close friends with his fellow scientists, to drink with them, dance with them, play with their children. By doing this, he had betrayed them. She said he had done damage to the freedoms they all enjoyed, in two ways: directly, by helping the Soviet Union, as was his intention; and also indirectly, by creating a climate of suspicion. Perhaps he had not thought of what he was doing to his friends.

He must now tell the security authorities who his contacts were, she said, to remove suspicion from other scientists, it is awfully hard, perhaps the hardest thing of all to do,' she wrote. 'But you went all the way in one direction, don't stop half-way now. You are not soft, and not one for the easy way out. You are a mathematician. This problem has no rigorous solution. Try to find the best approximation.'

Her next paragraph was harsher still. She said he could escape by committing suicide, but that would be to leave the mess behind him. His fate did not matter compared with his responsibility.

She concluded: 'You have burned your God. God help you.'

He replied quickly, writing with a scratchy pen on poor quality prison paper, so that there were blots and smudges. He admitted that he had not thought about the harm he was doing to his friends. 'I didn't, and that's the greatest horror I had to face when I looked at myself. You don't know what I had done to my own mind. I think I knew what I was doing, and there was this simple thing, obvious to the simplest decent creature, and I didn't think of it.' As for suicide, he said he had contemplated it as a way out, but had given it up by the time he was arrested.

He said he had learned to love again, and she had helped him.

His concluding paragraph was on a lighter note: 'I suppose you would almost enjoy the kind of thing I am learning about here. All these people in their way are kind and decent. Even the chap who apparently made prison his home, with occasional excursions to pick up a few hundred pounds and have a few riotous weeks on them. He grew quite sympathetic when I admitted that I hadn't made any money out of it. Nothing could shake him from the belief that I had been double-crossed.'

Erna Skinner wrote to him, and he replied, asking the Skinners to try to understand his point of view. These letters have been destroyed — Elaine Skinner burned them after her parents died — but one sentence from Fuchs's letter to Erna Skinner remains: 'Some people grow up at 15, some at 38. It is more painful at 38.'

She was shattered by the discovery of what he had been doing, and this undoubtedly contributed to the decline which led to bouts of heavy drinking and a nervous breakdown. When she talked about it, it was in the terms of someone whose world has suddenly been swept away. Once, she said: it was as if a series of horrible murders were committed in a community, and you suddenly found that it was your husband, or your neighbour, or your son, or somebody you trusted just like yourself. It was so unbelievable that once you grasped it, you looked at the world completely differently.'

Then the Peierls went to Brixton together to see Fuchs. They decided beforehand that there were three specific questions to which they wanted answers, and they dropped these into the conversation.

Why had he brought back Kravchenko's book *I Chose Freedom* from America as a present for Mrs Peierls? He said he was just curious to know what she would think of it. Why, since he was a spy, did he drink so much, and take the risk of giving away his secret? He said he was sure he could retain his self-control no matter how much he drank.

Most puzzling of all, how could he think of bringing his nephew over from Germany and adopting him? The boy had already had a very disturbed childhood. What effect would it have on him if he came to live with Fuchs and then Fuchs was arrested? Fuchs answered that he had not considered this because he had divided his mind into two compartments, and put all his espionage activities into one compartment, so that they simply did not touch other matters. By way of explanation, he used the phrase he had used in his confession to Skardon (which the Peierls had not yet seen): controlled schizophrenia.

On this and on several other occasions, Fuchs expressed his regret at having deceived his friends, and particularly Henry Arnold. The attachment to Arnold remained, and he assumed that Arnold felt it also. He wrote to Arnold a week after he was arrested:

'I suppose you must sometimes have felt very lonely during the last few months. If only I had not vacillated at first and made up my mind straight away, everything would have been much easier, and perhaps I might also have saved you some pain. I hope Skardon showed you the document I signed. I wrote it for several people, and you were one of them.'

He went on in the letter to ask Arnold to sell his two cars, the MG and the old car he had driven before, which he had not yet disposed of and which was now being used by someone else at Harwell. He was very precise about details: 'The new licence for the MG is in one of the pockets beside the dashboard. You might as well go through the various pockets, which contain maps. The Morris may not be licensed, unless Jones has taken one out; if not, it may be necessary to take out a short-term licence. You can of course recover any expense.'

***

As it happens, a first cousin of Fuchs on his mother's side, Gisela Wagner, was spending a term at a teacher-training college in Kent, and she visited him in Brixton.

Fuchs appeared in court again on 10 February. This time it was for a preliminary hearing before Sir Laurence Dunne, for the magistrate to decide whether the case would be sent for trial. Representatives of the whole world's press were present. Fuchs was in the dock, but he was not called upon to say anything. He seemed calm throughout.

By now, he had retained a firm of solicitors, and they had appointed a counsel to defend him, although the defence counsel did not have much to do at the hearing. The prosecutor, Christmas Humphreys, summed up the case against him, drawing on his own confession and the exchanges over the past weeks. Arnold was the first witness. He testified about their recent exchanges, including Fuchs's admission to him that he had given information to foreign agents.

It was not an interrogation in the normal sense since its purpose was simply to put on the record facts that were known already to the prosecution. Humphreys asked leading questions and Arnold usually gave monosyllabic answers. As:

'Did you introduce Skardon to Fuchs?'

'Yes.'

'Were further meetings arranged?'

'Yes.'

'On January 26, 1950, did Fuchs see you again before seeing Skardon?'

'Yes.' And so on.

The next witness was Skardon. There was the same kind of questioning, with Humphreys asking leading questions, although Skardon talked a little more. The questions covered Skardon's meetings with Fuchs leading up to his confession, and then Skardon summarized Fuchs's confession.

At the end of this cross-examination Fuchs's defence counsel, Thomson Halsell, asked Skardon one question:

'Would it be fair to say that since lunchtime on January 24th, the defendant has helped you and been completely co-operative in every way?'

'Yes,' replied Skardon.

Then Perrin went into the witness box, and was led through the gist of Fuchs's statement to him about what he had told Soviet agents. The form of this cross-examination was the same as that of Skardon's, with Humphreys putting the facts into the questions. As:

'On January 30th, did you meet Skardon and the accused?'

'Yes.'

'Did he admit that he had passed technology information relating to atomic research to the Communists?'

'Yes.'

At the end of the hearing, Dunne announced that Fuchs would be sent for trial at the Central Criminal Court, the Old Bailey, on 28 February.

Arnold's appearance in court as a witness for the prosecution did not diminish Fuchs's affection for him. He continued to write to him, and to regard him as a friend. Nor did Skardon's appearance diminish Fuchs's attachment to him.

Just as, when he decided to help the Russians he at first thought he would give them only his own work, and soon dropped that restriction, so now he told the British authorities everything and dropped his refusal to identify his contacts. He was taking it upon himself to give all the help he could to the Western side in the Cold War, as he had once taken it upon himself to give all the help he could to the Soviet Union. In his prison cell he told MI5 men everything he could about his contacts, recognition signals and meeting places, always talking either to Skardon or in Skardon's presence. He did not know his contacts by name, but he went through photographs with the MI5 men. In this way he identified his first contact, Alexander, as Simon Davidovitch Kremer, of the Soviet Embassy.

Once, when he was not sure exactly where certain meetings took place, Skardon took him out in a car with a driver to the parts of London where the meeting places were, so that he could locate them, and then they went back to Brixton.

He had all his self-control. He was calm and collected

throughout this period, and gave no hint to anyone that he thought he faced a death sentence.

CHAPTER SIX

Shortly after this, Perrin found himself discussing the details of Fuchs's crime in the Garrick Club, a gentlemen's club favoured by senior figures in the theatre, publishing and the bar. Fuchs's solicitors had retained Derek Curtis-Bennett, a leading criminal lawyer, to defend him. Curtis-Bennett telephoned Perrin and told him that he needed the full text of his confession and his account of what he had told the Russians. Perrin said he could not show him these for security reasons, but he would give him a summary of what they contained. So, in the way things are done, Curtis-Bennett invited him to dinner at his club, and in the oak-panelled dining-room there, festooned with theatrical paintings and drawings, Perrin showed him the parts of the confession to Skardon that were to be made public, and told him roughly what Fuchs had told the Russians. Curtis-Bennett said that since Fuchs had already confessed, he could only advise him to plead guilty, and try in court to minimize his offence.

In the trial at the Old Bailey, the leading figures in the British legal structure took part. The judge was the Lord Chief Justice, Lord Goddard, the senior judge in England, a man known among lawyers for his Conservative politics and his belief in retributive justice, a burly figure with rugged features in his scarlet and ermine robes of office. Sir Hartley Shawcross himself prosecuted; the General Election had taken place a week earlier and had returned the Labour Party to office, albeit with a greatly reduced majority, so he was still Attorney-General. The Duchess of Kent was among the spectators. So was Gisela Wagner, Fuchs's cousin.

Curtis-Bennett conferred with Fuchs in the cell below the courtroom. He told him he would do his best to minimize the offence, but warned him that he might have to expect the maximum penalty. 'You know what that is?' he added.

'Yes, I know. It's death,' said Fuchs.

Then Curtis-Bennett realized what Fuchs had been facing these past weeks. 'No, you bloody fool, it's fourteen years,' he told him. 'You didn't give secrets to an enemy, you gave them to an ally.' Whatever relief Fuchs felt at that moment, he did not show it.

The indictment contained four counts. The exchanges with the American Government on the charges to be brought that delayed Commander Burt had evidently ruled out the specific charge of passing secrets of Los Alamos in Santa Fe, perhaps because it was thought that it would be embarrassing to air this; at any rate, these four were quite sufficient to establish the crime of treason.

The four counts were:

That on a day in 1943 in the city of Birmingham for a purpose prejudicial to the safety or interests of the State he communicated to a person unknown information relating to atomic research which was calculated to be, or might have been, or was intended to be, directly or indirectly, useful to an enemy.

That on a day unknown between December 31, 1943 and August 1, 1944, he, being a British subject, in the city of New York, committed a similar offence.

That on a day unknown in February, 1945, he, being a British subject at Boston, Massachusetts, committed a similar offence; and that on a day in 1947 in Berkshire, he committed a similar offence.

Sir Hartley Shawcross, in the opening speech for the prosecution, said the case was as serious as any that had ever been prosecuted under this statute. Then he set out to quell in advance the kind of objections that were made to a heavy sentence in Nunn May's case. He said there was no doubt that the information communicated was likely to be of the utmost value to an enemy. The country to which the information was conveyed need not be an actual enemy. 'It is enough that the foreign country concerned should be a potential enemy, one which, owing to some unhappy change in circumstances, might become an actual enemy, although perhaps a friend at the time that the information was communicated. That country might never become an enemy. In this case, information was in fact conveyed to agents of the Soviet Union.'

Sir Hartley then said that strictly speaking, there was no need for him to go into the prisoner's motives. However, he went on, in the statement by Fuchs which formed the basis of the prosecution, the questions of motive were so inextricably mixed with questions of fact that in fairness to him, and as a warning to others, it was right to say some word about motives, which would explain some of the facts.

'The prisoner is a Communist,' he said, 'and that is at once the explanation and indeed the tragedy of this case. Quite apart from the great harm that the prisoner has done to the country he adopted and which adopted him, it is a tragedy that one of such high intellectual attainments as the prisoner possesses should have allowed his mental processes to become so warped by his devotion to Communism that, as he himself expresses it, he became a kind of controlled schizophrenic, the dominant half of his mind leading him to do things which the other part of his mind recognized quite clearly were wrong.'

He then gave a picture of monolithic international Communism, as it was at the time:

'In this country the number of Communists is fortunately very few, and it may be that a great number of those people who support the Communist movement believe, as the prisoner at one time apparently believed, misguidedly if sincerely, that that movement is seeking to build a new world. What they don't realize is that it is to be a world dominated by a single power and that the supporters of Communism, indoctrinated with the Communist belief, must become traitors to their own country in the interests — or what they are told are the interests — of the international Communist movement.

'My Lord, it is because of these facts that this brilliant scientist, as he is, now undoubtedly disillusioned and ashamed, came to place this country and himself in this terrible position.'

Sir Hartley went through Fuchs's career in some detail, illustrating it with readings from the confession he made to Skardon, in particular his explanation of why he went to the Russians in the first place, of how he divided his mind into two compartments, the 'controlled schizophrenia', and his doubts during the past years. Sir Hartley pointed out in conclusion that Fuchs had made the confession voluntarily while he was a free man, and since then had given the authorities all the help he could. (Those parts of the confession that were not read out in court were classified by the British authorities, although it is difficult to see why. They remained classified, along with other official papers concerning Fuchs, even when most official documents of that time were released to the public in 1980 under the thirty-year rule.)[xx]

Skardon was called as the only defence witness. Curtis-Bennett got him to confirm that until Fuchs confessed there was no evidence on which he could be prosecuted, and that he had acted on his own initiative in making the confession.

Curtis-Bennett, in his defence speech, began by recalling the desperate political background of Fuchs's youth in Germany, leading up to the burning of the Reichstag. 'This scientist, this scholarly man, read the news in the newspaper on the train the morning after it happened,' he said. 'He went underground, scarcely saving his own life, and came to this country in 1933 for the purpose of continuing his studies in order to fit himself out to be a scientist to help in the rebuilding of a Communist Germany, not to throw atom bombs at anybody, but to study physics... He pursued his peaceful studies, and had not the war come, he may have been a candidate for a Nobel Prize or a membership of the Royal Society rather than for gaol.'

Curtis-Bennett was apparently inadequately briefed, for he then said that Fuchs had never pretended that he was not a Communist. Lord Goddard pulled him up on this. 'I don't know whether you are suggesting that that was known to the authorities,' Goddard said.

Curtis-Bennett: 'I don't know, but he made no secret of the fact.'

Goddard: 'I don't suppose he proclaimed himself as a Communist when naturalized or taken into Harwell, or when he went to the USA.'

Curtis-Bennett: if I am wrong, the Attorney-General will correct me. It was on his records in this country at the Home Office that he was a member of the German Communist Party.'

Sir Hartley intervened: it was realized when he was examined by the Enemy Aliens Tribunal at the beginning of the war that he was a refugee from Nazi persecution because in Germany he had been a Communist. All the investigations at that time and since have not shown that he had any association whatever with British members of the Communist Party.' (Actually, there is no record that any official body in Britain knew that he was a Communist in Germany.)

Curtis-Bennett went on to say that anyone who knew anything about Communism would know that a Communist coming into possession of valuable information would always put his allegiance to Communism above all else. Then, of Fuchs:

'He had a sort of sieve in his mind about the information he would or would not give, and in count one, 1943 — '

Lord Goddard interrupted him: i have read this statement with very great care more than once. I cannot understand this metaphysical philosophy or whatever you like to call it. I am not concerned with it. I am concerned that this man gave away secrets of vital importance to this country. He stands before me as a sane man, and not relying on the disease of schizophrenia or anything else.'

Curtis-Bennett: if Your Lordship does not think that the state of mind a man acts under is relative to sentence—'

Lord Goddard: 'A man in this state of mind is one of the most dangerous that this country could have within its shores.'

Curtis-Bennett battled on against Lord Goddard's philistinism:

'I have to endeavour to put before Your Lordship this man as he is, knowing that Your Lordship is not going to visit him savagely but justly, both in the interests of the state and in the interests of this man, and I can only try to explain what Your Lordship has said you fail to understand. Though I fail in the end, I can do no more, but do it I must.

'There was acting in his mind a sieve whereby, with regard to the first count, he would only tell things he found out himself. He is a scientist, a pencil-and-paper man, and it is good to hear the Attorney-General say that it is not in his power to make an atom bomb and hand it over to the Russians, to give away a mighty secret of that sort. In 1943, he gave information about what he himself knew out of his own head. I am not going to confuse this case with long medical terms. He is not mad. He is sane. But he is a human being, and that is what I am trying to explain.'

He went on to say that this sieve in Fuchs's mind opened up to let a lot of information through during the time that Russia was fighting as an ally of Britain, when the first three of the four offences were committed, and closed up later. 'It would be difficult to see how, in 1943 and 1945, when America was helping our Russian ally, that information given to Russia would be prejudicial to the state... The change of political alignments is not the business of scientists, for scientists are not always politically wise. Their minds move along straight lines without the flexibility that some others have.'

This was his lawyer's defence, not Fuchs's own. Fuchs would probably not have admitted, let alone claimed, that he was a simple scientist lost in the complexities of changing international alignments. Also, unlike Nunn May, he never said in his defence that he helped Russia because Russia was an ally of Britain and America; his first loyalty was to Russia because he was a Communist.

Curtis-Bennett concluded by pointing out that Fuchs had confessed of his own free will. 'There you have this man being logical, in my submission. Having decided to tell everything, he tells everything, makes it about as bad for himself as he can, and provides the whole of the case against him in this court. There is not one piece of evidence produced in this case which is not the result of the written and oral statements he made to. Mr Skardon in December and January.'

There was no further evidence and no other witnesses. Lord Goddard then asked Fuchs whether he had anything to say. Fuchs sat impassively, wearing a brown suit with pens and pencils protruding from his top jacket pocket. Now he rose and spoke for the only time during his hearings, very softly, almost murmuring.

'My Lord, I have committed certain crimes for which I am charged, and I expect sentence. I have also committed some other crimes which are not crimes in the eyes of the law — crimes against my friends — and when I asked my counsel to put certain facts before you, I did not do it because I wanted to lighten my sentence. I did it in order to atone for those other crimes.

'I have had a fair trial, and I wish to thank you and my counsel and my solicitors. I also wish to thank the Governor and his staff at Brixton Prison for the considerate treatment they have given me.'

This was still the pride of one who insists-on being his own judge, and being answerable to his own laws.

Then, while Fuchs stood there in the dock, Lord Goddard summed up his crime and passed sentence.

'In 1933, fleeing from political persecution in Germany, you took advantage of the right and privilege of asylum which has always been the boast of this country to extend to people persecuted in their own country for political opinions.

'You have betrayed the hospitality and protection given to you with the grossest treachery. In 1942, in return for your offer to put at the service of this country the great gifts providence has bestowed upon you in scientific matters, you were granted British nationality.

'From that moment, regardless of your oath, you started to betray secrets of vital import for the purpose of furthering a political creed held in abhorrence by the vast majority of this country, your object being to strengthen that creed, which was then known to be inimical to all freedom-loving countries. There are four matters which seem to me the gravest aspect of your crime.

'First, by your conduct you have imperilled the right of asylum which this country has hitherto extended. Dare we now give shelter to political refugees who may be followers of this pernicious creed, and who may well disguise themselves to bite the hand that feeds them?

'Secondly, you have betrayed not only the projects and inventions of your own brain, for which this country was paying you and enabling you to live in comfort in return for your promise of secrecy, but you have also betrayed the secrets of other workers in this field of science, not only in this country but in the United States, and thereby might have caused the gravest suspicion to fall on those you falsely treated as friends and who were misled into trusting you.

'Thirdly, you might have imperilled the good relations between this country and the great American republic with whom His Majesty is allied.

'Fourthly, you have done irreparable and incalculable harm both to this land and to the United States, and you did it, as your statement shows, merely for the purpose of furthering your political creed.

'I am willing to assume that you have not done it for gain. Your statement shows the depth of self-deception into which people like yourself can fall. Your crime is only thinly differentiated from high treason. But in this country we observe rigidly the rule of law, and as, technically, it is not high treason, you are not tried for that offence.

'I have now to assess the penalty which it is right that I should impose. It is not so much for punishment that I impose it, for punishment to a man of your mentality means nothing. My duty is to safeguard this country. How can I be sure that a man of your mentality, as shown in the statement you have made, may not at any other minute allow some curious working in your mind to lead you further to betray secrets of the greatest possible value and importance to this land?

'The maximum sentence Parliament has ordained is fourteen years. That is the sentence I pass upon you.'

Fuchs stood still, expressionless, throughout. He remained still for some moments after Goddard had finished, until the uniformed prison officer behind him tapped him on the shoulder. Then he turned to go, but, remembering something, turned back, picked up some papers from the chair, patted them into a neat pile, put them in his jacket pocket, and walked downstairs to the cells below.

He was taken from there to WormWood Scrubs prison in West London where many long-term prisoners serve the first part of their sentence, before being assigned to the prison best suited to them.

The next day the official Soviet news agency Tass published a statement, *pro forma,* that the Soviet Government had no knowledge of Fuchs and none of its officials had been in contact with him.

***

Naturally, British newspapers commented on the regrettable crime, and people were dismayed; this was disloyalty, and by someone to whom Britain had given asylum. However, there was no wave of accusations of being soft on Communist subversion, no demand for the heads of those responsible. For one thing, as Prime Minister Attlee was to remind Parliament, the leaks dated back to the time when the Conservatives, now in opposition, headed the wartime coalition government, so if ministers were to take the blame it would have to be shared between the parties. But in any case, although this was the most intense period of the Cold War between the West and the Soviet bloc, and in a few months' time it would turn into a shooting war in Korea and British troops would be fighting alongside Americans, the British people as a whole did not feel as intensely engaged in the Cold War as the American people, and Russia was not seen quite so vividly as the enemy. This was partly a national disinclination to intensity and also, at this time, a disinclination to follow an American lead. But also, while most people disliked thoroughly the idea of a Communist dictatorship, anti-Communism was tempered by a residue of sentiment from the wartime alliance with Russia, and sympathy for Russia's suffering in a common cause. Many people on the Left still could not shed entirely a benign image of the Soviet Union, as a country that practised a kind of Socialism; Russia's support for anti-fascism in the Spanish Civil War shaded over into its leading role in the war against Nazi Germany (the interlude of the Nazi-Soviet Pact being buried out of sight of the memory).

A right-wing Conservative Member of Parliament, Sir Waldron Smithers, suggested in the light of the Fuchs case that the Communist Party should be outlawed, but this kind of suggestion was expected only from the fringe Right, and it was not taken seriously. A few other Members of Parliament questioned the number and role of Soviet diplomatic personnel in Britain.

Prime Minister Attlee made a statement on the Fuchs case in the House of Commons four days after the trial. It was on the first day of the first session of the new Parliament.

'It is a most deplorable and unfortunate incident,' Attlee said. 'Here we had a refugee from Nazi tyranny, hospitably entertained, who was secretly working against the safety of this country. I say "secretly" because there is a great deal of loose talk in the Press suggesting inefficiency on the part of the security services. I entirely deny that.

'Not long after this man came into this country — that was in 1933 — it was said that he was a Communist. The source of that information was the Gestapo. At that time the Gestapo accused everybody of being a Communist. When the matter was looked into there was no support for this whatever. And from that time on there was no support. A proper watch was kept at intervals.'

He summarized Fuchs's career in Britain and the United States, and went on: 'In the autumn of last year, information came from the United States suggesting that there had been some leakage while the British mission, of which Fuchs was a member, was in the United States. This information did not point to any individual. The security services got to work and were, as the House knows, successful... I take full responsibility for the efficiency of the security services, and I am satisfied that unless we had here the kind of secret police they have in totalitarian countries, and employed their methods, which are reprobated rightly by everyone in this country, there was no means by which we could have found out about this man.'

He said the security services had acted 'promptly and effectively', and went on: i say that because it is very easy when a thing like that occurs — it was an appalling thing to have happened — to make assertions. I do not think any blame for what occurred attaches either to the Government of the right honourable gentleman opposite or to this Government or any of the officials. I think we had here a quite exceptional case.' Linking his own government with that of Sir Winston Churchill, 'the right honourable gentleman opposite' (Churchill since his election defeat in 1945 had been leader of the opposition), was a shrewd move to deflect criticism.

In the House of Lords the Lord Chancellor, Lord Jowett, also made a statement exonerating the security services. 'It may be asked why Fuchs was not detected earlier,' he said. 'Look at the facts, my lords. Fuchs had recruited himself. There was no time when he was undergoing training in conspiratorial technique during which our security services might have had an opportunity of detecting him. When he first offered himself to the Russians, he had all the accomplishments of an experienced spy; and for two years of his career he was in the

United States, beyond the reach of our counter-espionage services. And he has admitted that for another whole year, 1946, he had made no contact at all with his Russian masters or their intermediaries.'

Jowett said that tracking down Fuchs was 'a really brilliant achievement', and he went on: 'It should be plainly understood both here and abroad that so far from our security services having anything to apologize for in this case, I am quite satisfied that they have every reason to be proud of the work they did and the way in which they did it.

'There is no reason whatever to fear that secrets which are entrusted to our officers are in the least likely to be broken. A case of that sort might occur anywhere, whatever system is employed, if the man concerned is clever enough and wicked enough.'

It seems that the sentence about 'secrets which are entrusted to our officers' was aimed at the United States, for there was concern in Britain at the effect that the case would have on British-American exchanges of secret information. There were good grounds for this concern.

***

When Sir John Cockcroft sailed off on the *Queen Elizabeth* the previous November, happy to be turning his back on the painful question of Fuchs's loyalty, he was on his way to Washington along with William Penney to meet American and Canadian officials, to discuss a new plan to revive wartime co-operation on the production of atomic bombs. The discussions would be in the framework of a meeting of the Combined Development Agency. This and the Declassification Committee were the only institutions left over from wartime co-operation in this area. The agency existed only to organize the supply of uranium, but its meeting was a convenient place to discuss the new plan. Cockcroft had every reason to feel optimistic.

The proposal came from the State Department, although it was something the British Government had wanted for a long time. It would have meant sharing research and development, with the British seconding some scientists to Los Alamos, as they had done during the war.

President Truman gave the plan his backing, and in July, Truman and other Administration officials met with a few senior members of Congress to brief them on the plan and ask for their support. State Department officials pointed out at the meeting that Britain was intending to produce its own atomic bombs anyway, and had the ability to do so. The senators and congressmen were sympathetic on the whole. Some said they were worried about sharing America's unique knowledge of the atomic bomb with anyone, but this argument was largely stilled when Russia exploded its atomic bomb in September.

The plan was received favourably at the tripartite meeting in Washington in November. The following month, the British ambassador, Sir Oliver Franks, discussed the prospect of congressional approval with Dean Acheson, the Secretary of State, in an after-dinner chat. He cabled the Foreign Office: 'Acheson said it should be possible to get Congress to make the necessary changes in the law, provided that an agreement could be demonstrated to produce maximum results in the most efficient way.'

The British Cabinet discussed the proposals at a meeting on 30 December, and approved them.

Then came Fuchs's arrest, and cables from the Washington embassy reflected anxiety. One said: 'We are receiving criticism even from normally friendly quarters for our laxity and "ideological blindness".' Sir Oliver Franks cabled a summary of Press comment after Fuchs's trial and said: 'This report contains further evidence of the damage done to our prestige by the Fuchs case. Criticism of what is called our "laxity" is widespread. Some responsible newspapers are arguing vigorously against any curtailment of Anglo-American exchanges of atomic information; but it is the mood of Congress that matters most.'

It was indeed. Acheson recorded in his memoirs the outcome of his effort to achieve a new agreement on cooperation in atomic weapons: 'Then a bomb exploded in London. A British scientist — Klaus Fuchs, who had been working in this country on the Manhattan Project during the war — was arrested, and charged with passing on to the Russians information he had acquired then and later. In due course he was tried and convicted. Also in February, Senator McCarthy began his attacks on the State Department. The talks with the British and Canadians returned to square one, where there was a deep freeze from which they did not return in my time.'

Two months later, Acheson recalled, he visited London and met Attlee and other government leaders. 'Attlee wanted to know whether there was any way of reviving the talks that had been interrupted by the Fuchs affair... I said regretfully that the effort I had tried so hard to pilot into safe waters had foundered, and I doubted that it would ever rise again.'[xxi]

It is given to few scientists to have so direct an influence on the course of international relations as Fuchs had.

The influence of the case did not stop there. A year later, in February 1951, scientific attaché Alec Longair cabled the Foreign Office from the Washington embassy concerning scientific and technical co-operation in general: 'The arrest and conviction of Klaus Fuchs had effects which went very deep indeed. It is easy to blame everything on this, but the truer position is that a technical co-operation programme which was not working well before Fuchs's arrest is now working very badly. It should be remembered that we for our part have gone very cautiously in making suggestions since the Fuchs business.'

For the revelation of Fuchs's espionage came just at the time when it was likely to have the greatest impact on the United States. Americans were preoccupied at this time with the Cold War. America was still reeling, figuratively speaking, from the shock of the Communist victory in the Chinese Civil War, which joined China to what was then the Soviet Bloc, and the more recent news that Russia could now threaten the United States with atomic bombs. Communism was seen as a threat from within as well as without, and anti-Communist hysteria and spy fever were growing. This was the beginning of the time of loyalty oaths and blacklists, and the withdrawal of passports from suspected radicals, which was later declared illegal by the Supreme Court. (Edward Corson's passport was taken away from him as he was about to sail for France, after he had sent that cable to Fuchs assuring him that he believed in his innocence. It was given back to him only after he explained his position.) Clamorous voices on the far Right were blaming setbacks in American policy on spies and traitors: the Communist victory in China on Communist sympathizers among the old China hands in the State Department, the Soviet presence in Eastern Europe on Alger Hiss and State Department liberals. As Acheson indicated in his memoirs, Senator Joseph McCarthy began his notorious career as an anti-Communist demagogue in February 1950, the month in which Fuchs was arrested, with his famous speech before an audience in Wheeling, West Virginia, in which he brandished before them a sheaf of papers which he claimed was a list of 200 Communists in the State Department. With the Fuchs case, this current of irrationality mingled inextricably with reasonable concerns over security.

Arthur Krock, the senior Washington columnist of the *New York Times,* said the case was 'a bombshell' in official Washington, and added that it 'has had an impact, and a powerful one, on the entire government of the United States, for reasons which stretch far beyond the interests of national security'.

The witch-hunters of the Right felt confirmed in their views.

Senator Homer Capehart said: 'There are other spies too, and there will continue to be so long as we have a President who refers to such matters as "red herrings" and a Secretary of State who refuses to turn his back on Alger Hiss.' (This referred to two off-the-cuff remarks that were widely quoted.) Senator John Bricker said: 'I've always opposed the use of foreign scientists on atomic projects. The arrest of Fuchs makes me even more certain that I am right about this.'

The Joint Senate-House Committee on Atomic Energy began hearings in secret to find out how much information had been given to the Russians. The British sent them the full text of Fuchs's confession, including the parts that were not read out in open court, and also his account to Perrin of what he had told the Russians. The Chairman, Senator Brian McMahon, told reporters that he had been shocked before he saw these documents, and now he was even more shocked. The Committee were anxious most of all to know how much Fuchs knew about the super, the hydrogen bomb that was now to be developed. After all, Russia already had a fission bomb now.

Senator McMahon said they were considering asking for Fuchs to be extradited so that he could stand trial in America for acts of espionage that he had committed in America, but the Committee's counsel advised them that Fuchs's breach of domestic British law took precedence, and that the British Government would not extradite him.

The Chairman of the Atomic Energy Commission, David Lilienthal, gave the Committee a sombre account of the damage that Fuchs could have done, emphasizing that he was at the centre of things at Los Alamos and would have known most of what there was to know. But he also advised them: 'Let's not panic the country. Keep your shirt on. Don't wallow in it. And let's hope this won't disturb the Los Alamos outfit, or investigations so harass everyone that the new super programme is held up.' Like a number of other people, he was worried that the case might give more impetus to witch-hunts.

He had cause to worry, for the case was indeed used to further political and personal ends.

President Truman had followed his statement of 10 January about developing the hydrogen bomb with an announcement on 10 March that he had instructed the Atomic Energy Commission to 'continue work' on it, meaning that it was not only going to be developed but produced (although no one knew how to produce a hydrogen bomb or even whether it could be done). He had been under considerable pressure from some members of the AEC, and others, to make this announcement, and go all out to build the hydrogen bomb as soon as possible. Five days after this, one of the AEC members who had urged him to make the announcement, Admiral Lewis Strauss, talked on the telephone with J. Edgar Hoover, the Director of the FBI, about Fuchs's statement, which he had just seen. As Hoover recorded in a memorandum immediately after this conversation, Strauss said that if these statements were published, 'It will very much reinforce the hand of the President on the strength of the decision he made a few days ago.'

Strauss also asked Hoover to look into any links between Fuchs and the Institute for Advanced Study at Princeton, New Jersey. The Director of the Institute was Robert Oppenheimer, who was also now Chairman of the Atomic Energy Commission's General Advisory Committee. He was Strauss's principal opponent in the argument over whether the United States should develop the hydrogen bomb now — Oppenheimer and his committee had advised against it — and on other issues.

Strauss was not alone in trying to use the Fuchs case to get at Oppenheimer. The Executive Director of the Joint Senate-House Atomic Energy Committee was William Borden. He noted in a letter to Strauss that Fuchs had indicated that the Russians had another source of information at Los Alamos; Borden had someone in mind. Later, when he left the

Committee to take a job in business, he spelled it out, and wrote to Hoover that Oppenheimer was 'more probably than not an agent of the Soviet Union'. This letter set off the process that ended in the Oppenheimer hearings and the removal of his security clearance, an event that was for many Americans a climax of the assaults on the liberal intellectuals.

The FBI found that it already had Fuchs's Communist past on record but no one had noticed it, and the FBI, understandably, did not point it out now. The information was in Gestapo files that were brought to the United States in 1945, and indexed in 1948. On the eve of Germany's invasion of Russia, the Gestapo had drawn up a list of 5,000 Germans associated with pro-Soviet or Communist activities. One entry read: 'Fuchs, Klaus, student of philosophy, born 29 December 1911, Russelsheim, RSHA IVA, Gestapo Field Office, Kiel. (RSHA stands for Central Office of Security Police.) In these days of computerized files, this one would have interacted with others, such as a list of participants in the atom bomb project, and would almost certainly have come to the attention of the security authorities.

The FBI initiated a massive search for Fuchs's American contact or contacts. They had very little to go on besides Fuchs's description, which had been given to them by the British authorities.

They sought out Kristel Heineman, since she had seen the man in her home. But she was now a patient at the Westboro State Mental Hospital in Massachusetts. She had been admitted the previous April, and was diagnosed as suffering from schizophrenia and dementia praecox.

Doctors allowed FBI agents to interview her briefly. She told them that Albert Einstein had sent for her brother to help work on the atomic bomb. Einstein had played no part in the bomb project — although he signed the letter to Roosevelt that first alerted the US Government to the possibility — he did not know Fuchs, and this statement was obviously the product of a disordered mind. (She also told the FBI men that she had a lover who was the father of all three of her children.) None the less, Einstein was identified with liberal causes, and FBI headquarters in Washington instructed the Boston office to ask both Robert and Kristel Heineman for 'all info in their possession re any relationship between Fuchs and Dr Albert E. Einstein'.

FBI agents got to Harry Gold eventually following a lead given by Elizabeth Bentley, a self-confessed courier for a spy network, and one of a number of people who achieved notoriety in that strange time by naming other people as Soviet agents. She named a lot — ninety altogether — but in most cases no corroborative evidence was found, and in no case was the person named convicted of espionage. One person she named was Abraham Brothman, who owned a firm of industrial chemists, and he was brought before a grand jury. Brothman said he had contacted Soviet officials only in an effort to get export orders from the Soviet Government, and denied any wrongdoing. Harry Gold, who was an employee of his, gave evidence supporting his story.

The FBI noted that Fuchs had recalled that his contact had some scientific knowledge and might be a chemist, and also that he might have said something about living in Philadelphia. (Fuchs's physical description of his contact did not tally closely with Gold; Gold was older and taller than Fuchs remembered him.) FBI agents visited Gold's home in Philadelphia and questioned him, one of a great many calls on people they made in the course of their search.

Gold said he had never handled espionage material, had never met Fuchs, had never been to Santa Fe to see him, and in fact, had never been west of the Mississippi in his life. He was co-operative, and told the FBI men they were welcome to search his home. Carrying out the search, one of them found a map that had fallen behind a bookcase; it was a street map of Santa

Fe, the one he had bought in preparation for his meeting there with Fuchs. Confronted with this, Gold confessed that he was Raymond.

Meanwhile, Hoover had asked the British authorities for permission to send FBI agents to interview Fuchs in prison. A peremptory request to the Home Office delivered before Fuchs was brought to trial was peremptorily refused. A later request, delivered more diplomatically through the American Embassy in London, was granted. It says something of the anti-American atmosphere in Britain at this time, brought on partly by the antics of the anti-Communist witch-hunters with whom the FBI was identified, that objections were raised in Parliament to this. One member, George Thomas, said: 'This distasteful procedure is watched with some anxiety by the public.' The Home Secretary, Chuter Ede, had to assure the House that permission had been granted only because of the special circumstances of this case, and that Fuchs would be interviewed only if he was willing.

Two FBI agents, Hugh H. Clegg and Robert J. Lamphere, set out from the Washington office. On the way to New York, where they were to catch their plane, they stopped in Philadelphia to collect some photographs and movie film taken of Gold. He had not yet confessed at this time, but he was under surveillance. The film was taken clandestinely, from a car.

They interviewed Fuchs ten times altogether, between 20 May and 2 June, in a room in Wormwood Scrubs prison normally reserved for prisoners' consultations with their lawyers. Sometimes the interview lasted only an hour, sometimes it lasted longer with a break for lunch. Skardon was present at every one.

The first began with Fuchs asking the FBI men some questions. He asked about his friend Edward Corson. He told them. Corson knew nothing about his espionage activities, and wanted an assurance that Corson was not in any trouble because he had sent that cable after he was arrested. They told him that Corson was not under suspicion. Then he asked about Kristel Heineman, his sister. They assured him that the FBI men who questioned her had conferred with her doctors first, and that they were concerned not to aggravate her condition.

Clegg and Lamphere took up right away the question of the identity of Fuchs's American contact, 'Raymond'. He gave them as full a description as he could, much as he had done already for the British intelligence service. Then the two agents showed him fourteen photographs of several different people, and he picked out three pictures of Gold as possibles.

At the next interview they had a projector, and they showed the film of Gold. Fuchs was trying hard. The film was taken in secret and was not all that clear. 'I cannot be very positive, but I think that it's very likely him,' he said. 'There are certain mannerisms I seem to recognize, such as the too obvious way he has of looking around and looking back.' At a later interview, they showed the film again, and also some new photographs of Gold which had just been flown to London. He looked at these, and said finally, 'Yes, that's my American contact.' He confirmed this when he saw the film again. At their request, he wrote on the photograph, in scratchy, irregular handwriting: 'I identify this photograph as the likeness of the man whom I knew under the name of Raymond, (signed) Klaus Fuchs, 26th May, 1950.'

The FBI did not wait for this final identification to arrest Gold: he had already confessed and they arrested him in Philadelphia on the same day that Fuchs wrote this statement. Fuchs's positive identification was taken as corroboration.

Then, over the next few interviews, Fuchs took Clegg and Lamphere through all his contacts, recalling everything he could about people, places, dates, details, in Britain as well as America. He was hazy about some details, particularly the meeting with Gold in Cambridge, Massachusetts, in February 1945. He also recalled what he had told Raymond. He even recounted in detail his trip to America in 1947.

At the end of these interviews, they engaged in an exercise which shows something of the atmosphere of suspicion in America at this time. They went through a long list of his scientific colleagues, including Oppenheimer. Fuchs told them the extent of his friendship with each one. They reported each faithfully, and added to each that Fuchs knew of no 'Communist or espionage activities' by this person.

***

Fuchs continued to correspond with Arnold, his friend and his hunter, his cherished nemesis. In one letter, written nearly six weeks after his arrival in Wormwood Scrubs, he wrote:

> I want to thank you very much for all the trouble you are taking looking after my belongings. In some way I can't feel that they belong to me, since most of it is so much a part of my life at Harwell. For that reason, if there is anything you or the Skinners or Rennies would like to have please take it — not as a gift, but as something that rightly belongs to you.
> The book which I would like to have is the third edition of Einstein's *The Meaning of Relativity*.
> I believe I still owe the Rennies some money for milk and rations etc. Could you please ask Marjorie and settle it?

After this, he tried again, with Arnold's help, to search in his heart and mind, to work out the meaning of what he had done and its significance for his own character:

> I think it was better that Skardon handled the matter, because I would be certain that my decisions were really my own, and not made because of mental stress. When first you told me that you *[word illegible]* about it, I was already prepared to go

through with it, even though Skardon, I suppose, was not yet sure about it.

What I am trying to say, and I haven't succeeded very well, is that you must not blame yourself for anything that you did. Blame me — and if you can't do that, blame Hitler and Karl Marx and Stalin and their blasted company.

However, the real hurt is much farther back. How could I deceive in this way? I am not trying to excuse — in fact I am trying hard to understand it myself — because it hurts me too. I know I got myself to the point when I myself did not know that I was deceiving you, whilst I was actually doing it. Sometimes I knew it immediately afterwards, when you praised me, and those were the worst moments. But usually I could go on for days and weeks.

Then he went on to explain his drinking, in a passage quoted earlier:

Mrs Peierls asked me today:[xxii] how could you drink the way you did? As a matter of fact, it did surprise me when I found that I could get drunk without any fear. I thought at the time that even then I could control myself, but I don't think that explanation is correct. I think the truth is that under the influence of alcohol the control disappeared, but not only the control but also the whole other compartment of my mind. Does it make sense? And if it does make sense, if just a little alcohol could turn it into schizophrenia, how far gone was I in my 'normal' life?

I don't dare yet to pretend that I really know the answer to these questions. But I think that I am getting nearer to it every day. You can help me — if you are frank with me, without fear of hurt.

Please give my love to Eva [Arnold's wife].

In another letter, he told Arnold he had been reading Charles Dickens's *A Tale of Two Cities*, and had been 'bowled over' by the first paragraph:

> It was the best of times, it was the worst of times, it was the age of wisdom, it was the age of foolishness, it was the epoch of belief, it was the epoch of incredulity, it was the season of Light, it was the season of Darkness, it was the spring of hope, it was the winter of despair, we had everything before us, we had nothing before us...

Evidently Fuchs, who liked clear-cut answers, was powerfully impressed by this depiction of opposites coexisting.

Fuchs was searching to find what it was within himself that enabled him to ignore so boldly the normal requirements of relationships with other people, to divide his mind in the way that he did, and keep reality at bay. He felt some trepidation, as anyone must who conducts such a search seriously.

We don't know enough to understand his inner motivations, but we can see some areas of his mind and his life where the motivations that he did not understand may have developed. Fuchs said his childhood was a very happy one. But the experience of psychiatrists is that a person may not be a good judge of whether or not his childhood was happy. His memory may bend itself to meet some requirements in his mind, something that says he *ought* to recall a happy childhood (or an unhappy one in some cases). A family in which the three women members suffer two suicides and a mental illness contains dark areas, remembered or not.

It would be interesting to know what Fuchs's relationship with his mother was before she committed suicide. And what his reactions were to the event: Grief? Pity? Loss? Guilt? Relief? Why was this woman who was his mother for nineteen years apparently so remote from his recollection? In subsuming his emotions and replacing them with political beliefs — for even as a student in Germany, he chose his friends from his political comrades, his affections following ideological lines — he would be able to suppress feelings about his mother along with others.

Emil Fuchs wrote about his wife Else in his memoirs with respect, but he did not write about her very much; in fact, she hardly features in them at all. The traditional German family has a strong, authoritarian father and a soft, compliant mother. In this family, the mother seems almost to be absent.

Emil Fuchs does not seem like an authoritarian figure. Decent, humane, concerned for others, brave, he encouraged his children to form their own beliefs and find their own ways, yet somehow, they all went most of the distance along his way. Parents instruct their children on a verbal, conscious level and at the same time on another, unconscious level. Sometimes, those two sets of instructions contradict one another. A family, or any other close-knit group, may have relationships on both of these levels, the one conscious and visible, the other unconscious and observable only by the effects it creates, like sub-atomic particles.

The picture that emerges of the Fuchs family is cloudy and of necessity very incomplete. It is of a family in which extraordinary pressures are felt by the women, the mother and two daughters, but apparently not by the father and two sons; two of these, at least, have strong personalities and lead successful lives. But the mother seems to be partially erased from the memories of these two. The father appears to be permissive, yet the effect is as if he had issued commands and had been obeyed, as if, in fact, on one level he *was* commanding. It seems almost as if he played the roles of both parents in the traditional German family, replacing the mother.

The second son, Klaus, is highly intelligent, closely attached to other members of the family, but, as regards the outside world, very independent. He is able to establish relationships of mutual affection and support while remaining on one level detached.

He follows his father's precepts all his life. He has women friends: one is a 'spoiler of men', another his 'English mother'. But he does not form a strong, exclusive sexual bond with a woman, nor even, it appears, acknowledge the need for one, until comparatively late in life, when as we shall see he has returned to the country that is both his father's land and his fatherland. (Britain, by contrast, is always the mother country.) He has a powerful, even dominant, sense of right and wrong. In Freudian terms, one can say that he has a very strong super-ego, and an id that is almost buried out of sight.

Speculations along these lines should not be taken as an attempt to explain away Fuchs's political beliefs, to invalidate them by describing them in terms of unconscious motivations. He deserves to have his belief in Communism and his later change of mind treated at his own assessment. For one thing, they parallel the changing beliefs of a lot of other people during this period. His story belongs to the real world of politics and ethics.

His crime was treason. But it cannot be answered simply by an appeal to patriotism. Other causes besides Communism are international. No democrat would have blamed Fuchs because, while a German citizen, he helped the war effort against Nazi Germany, nor would a democrat accept an accusation of treason against Soviet citizens who oppose the Communist system. Today there is a possibility of a war that threatens not merely one nation, but the planet, the whole biosphere. Many major issues — in fact, all the really major issues — transcend national boundaries. Now, more than ever, patriotism is not enough.

Fuchs was not motivated in what he did by ambition, or greed. He was selfless. More than most people, he was driven by a moral passion to do what is right. His dilemma was one of conflicting loyalties.

One can require loyalty, but one cannot command it. It would have been wrong for the British authorities to have rejected Fuchs simply because he had once been a member of the

German Communist Party (although they would have had good grounds for suspecting him because he concealed the fact). A former attachment to Communism, or some other alternative to our form of government, cannot be taken in itself as an indicator of potential treason. It is not unusual for intelligent young people in particular to look at different ways of organizing society, and to prefer one radically different from their own, and perhaps even opposed to it, nor is it unusual for them to change their minds later on. A woman can demand of her husband that he should not be unfaithful to her, and *vice versa.* She cannot reasonably demand of him that he never find any other woman attractive. If she is going to make this requirement, she would do best to marry either a blind man or a liar. *Mutatis mutandis,* if a government requires as a criterion of loyalty unswerving lifelong support for its system, then a lot of people who satisfy this condition will be either fools or good liars.

Loyalty has an exclusive quality. Whether the requirement for it is embodied in an oath of allegiance or a marriage vow, it involves pledging a fidelity to one that is denied to others. A conflict of loyalty arises because two loyalties are mutually exclusive. This is a perennial theme in literature, a conflict between love and duty, or friend and country. And not only in literature: such conflicts occur in real life. Whether something is loyal or treacherous may depend on the perspective. During the Algerian War, when elements in the French Government were trying to curb some of the brutal methods that the army was employing to put down the rebellion, officers of one paratroop regiment took a secret oath on the Bible that if they were questioned by a tribunal about the torture of Arab suspects, they would not tell the truth. They were being resolutely loyal to the men they led, but false to their government; they were taking a solemn oath to break another. During the Watergate goings-on, Deep Throat leaked information about the dirty dealings in the circle around Nixon because, presumably, he rated loyalty to certain standards of conduct, or perhaps to the law, above loyalty to the President.

There is another instance of conflicting loyalties that is more directly pertinent to the case of Klaus Fuchs. It has never been told in print before.

During World War II, an American Air Force officer stationed in Britain somehow picked up a sketchy idea of a secret weapon programme that seems to have been the atomic bomb project. He thought, wrongly, that this was an American project from which Britain was excluded, and about which the British Government knew nothing. He evidently brooded on the morality of this, and then decided to act. By pulling strings, he got an appointment with the Chief of the RAF, Air Chief Marshal Sir John Portal. He told Portal that since arriving in Britain, he had been very impressed by the suffering that the British people had endured in the war and the fortitude with which they had borne this. Then he said that his government, the American Government, was engaged on a programme to build an important new weapon and was keeping this secret from Britain, its ally. He thought this was wrong, and he wanted -

At this point, Portal stood up and said, 'Get out of this office at once! If you say another word, I'll call your superior officer and have you arrested and court martialled.'[xxiii]

Clearly, Portal was right. Certainly his was a military man's natural reaction. The American officer had no right to disobey orders and take it upon himself to reverse his government's actions. He was being disloyal to his government and his oath of loyalty as an officer. But many people would at least sympathize with his motives. Even Portal did, to the extent of sparing him arrest and court martial.

Certainly Emil Fuchs saw it that way. Some time after his son was sent to prison, he told the writer Robert Jungk that he had 'the highest respect' for his son's decision to do what he did, and he went on: 'He was justly condemned under British law. But there must always be from time to time people who deliberately assume such guilt as his... They have to take the consequences of their resolute affirmation that they see a position more clearly than those who have the power, at that juncture, to deal with it. Should it not be clear by this time that my son acted with more accurate foresight in the interests of the British people than did their government?'[xxiv]

Fuchs broke promises that he had given freely, his promise of secrecy when he joined the atomic bomb project and his oath of allegiance to the British Crown, and betrayed a trust that others had placed in him. This is treachery. This kind of betrayal corrodes the bonds that bind people to one another, and pollutes the social environment with mistrust.

Yet most of us, like Emil Fuchs, place a high value on individual morality, and the right of each person to work out for himself what is right and wrong. This is one of the great achievements of Western humanism. Because we do, we take a chance that someone will decide, as Fuchs did, that any degree of betrayal is justified in this or that higher cause. The risk of a Klaus Fuchs every now and again is a price we pay for individualism.

After the defection to Moscow of another Harwell scientist, Bruno Pontecorvo, and the trial and conviction of Julius and Ethel Rosenberg, the Joint Congressional Committee on Atomic Energy examined all the cases of which came to be called atomic espionage. Their report, in April 1951, rated Fuchs by far the most important, and said: 'It is hardly an exaggeration to say that Klaus Fuchs alone has influenced the safety of more people and accomplished greater damage than any other spy, not only in the history of the United States, but in the history of nations.' The report also said: 'If the United States had known early in World War II what Russia had learned by 1945 through espionage, it would have saved eighteen months.'

Others have come to a similar conclusion. Rudolf Peierls was at an international physics conference once and was chatting with a Russian physicist who had worked on the Soviet atomic bomb. He asked him how much difference Fuchs's information had made. The man said he would like to consult a couple of his colleagues before answering. Then he came back and said they decided it had saved Russia between one and two years.

One cannot say how much if at all the world changed because Russia acquired the atomic bomb sooner than it would have otherwise. A Federal judge in New York City, Judge Irving Saypol, sentenced the Rosenbergs to death because, he said, North Korea would not have started the Korean War if Russia did not have the atomic bomb, and so the Rosenbergs were partly responsible for the deaths of the Americans who were killed in Korea. This is certainly possible, but it is speculation.[xxv]

Certainly if Russia's acquisition of the atomic bomb was linked to the outbreak of the Korean War, then Fuchs was the person in the West who was principally responsible.

There was one more blow in store for Fuchs. In December 1950 the British Deprivation of Citizenship Committee said it proposed to take away his citizenship. Under the British Nationality Act 1948, Section 10, Subsection A, a person having been naturalized can be deprived of his citizenship 'if he has shown himself by act or speech to be disloyal or disaffected towards His Majesty'. Before this can be done, a hearing must be held, and the person has the right to speak. The final decision rests with the Home Secretary.

Sir Hartley Shawcross gave evidence before the committee, and said that the only consideration in the question was 'whether it is in the public interest that Fuchs should continue as a British subject'.

Fuchs did not avail himself of his right to appear before the committee, but he wrote a letter arguing that his citizenship should not be taken away, and this was read out.

He wrote:

> If this was intended as punishment for my actions, there would be little that I could say except that I have already received the maximum sentence permissible by law. However, section 20 of the British Nationality Act 1948, to which you refer, appears to exclude the intention of punishment. I assume, therefore, that the question under consideration is my present and future loyalty.
>
> Lest silence on my part should be interpreted as an indication that even now I do not appreciate the values and obligations of citizenship of this country, I wish to submit the following representations to the Secretary of State.[xxvi]
>
> 1 cannot expect the Secretary of State to accept an assurance of loyalty from me. However, I wish to submit that — in order to determine the matter in a judicial manner — the Secretary of State should obtain the opinion of those Government departments which have been concerned with my case, that is, M15 and the Director of Public Prosecutions.
>
> My disloyal actions ceased early in 1949 before any suspicion had been voiced against me. I had received no relevant promise and no substantial threat. I was not forced to confess by any evidence.
>
> I think the facts mentioned would have been of great value in a plea in mitigation. I have loyally co-operated with MI5 and the FBI although no threat or promise has been made to me at any time before or after my trial.
>
> I submit that these facts show that in making my confession and in my subsequent actions, I was guided by my convictions and loyalties, and that they show clearly where my loyalties are.

Despite this plea, the Committee recommended that his

citizenship be taken away from him, and this was done. Fuchs thought he had found a home, and now he was expelled.

Skardon still used to visit him in prison; M15 wanted to keep in touch with him in case new questions arose which he might be able to answer. But now Fuchs told Skardon that their friendship, as he called it, was ended. 'If you were a policeman and I was arrested for burglary,' he said to him, 'and I came clean and gave you all the help I could, I would expect you to do all you could to help me.' Skardon protested that he could not have stopped the committee taking away his British nationality, but Fuchs told him he did not want to see him any more.

After three months at Wormwood Scrubs, he was transferred to Stafford Prison, where he sewed mailbags, and then six months later, to Wakefield Prison in Yorkshire. This is a prison for long-term prisoners, many of them, in the nature of things, violent criminals. As an eminent criminal much written about in the newspapers, he had considerable status among the prisoners when he arrived, and was treated with respect.

The long-term prisoners at Wakefield had individual cells, so he did not share one. He behaved in prison much as he did outside. He was quiet, reserved and self-contained; he did not mix much. He occasionally played chess with other prisoners, and because he was a skilful player he used to start without a queen, to give his opponent the advantage, but still he always won. A few prisoners doing correspondence courses in physics or maths asked his help, and he gave it. He also wrote some articles explaining physics in simple terms for the Wakefield Prison magazine, and acquired the nickname 'the Doc'. He was assigned congenial work in the prison library.

He used to read a lot, particularly Marxist classics. He had some long talks on philosophical questions with one of the assistant governors, Gordon Hawkins, who had a degree in philosophy and did postgraduate work in the subject at Balliol

College, Oxford. Fuchs would expound the philosophy of dialectical materialism. He gave Hawkins *In Defence of Materialism* by Georgi Plekhanov, one of the classics of Marxist philosophy, to read and they discussed it.

They talked about world affairs as well as philosophy. Fuchs followed the Rosenbergs' case, and when they were sentenced to death he remarked that he was lucky that he had not been convicted in America; there, he would have been executed.

He noted Sir Winston Churchill's famous depiction in 1955 of the thermonuclear balance of terror, after both America and Russia had exploded a hydrogen bomb: 'A paradox has emerged. Let me put it simply. After a certain point has been passed, the worse things get, the better. The broad effect of the latest development is to spread almost indefinitely, or at least to a great extent, the area of mortal danger... Then it may well be that, by a process of sublime irony, we shall have reached a stage in this story where safety will be the sturdy child of terror, and survival the twin brother of annihilation.'

Fuchs pointed this out to Hawkins, and said, 'I suppose the process of sublime irony won't extend to my being released, as a benefactor of the human race.' It was a wry joke. Fuchs, by helping the Russians build the atomic bomb, had certainly done his bit to put balance into the terror.

When the first sputnik went up, and there was some fanciful talk of the exploration of space and putting men on the moon, Fuchs explained to Hawkins lucidly and patiently why this was impossible. You might send a rocket to the moon, he explained, but you could not bring a vehicle back because of the heat that would be generated when a fast-moving object hits the Earth's atmosphere. He even made some rough calculations to demonstrate the point. Once again, he had underestimated the resources of modern technology. He could foresee the re-entry problem, but not that it would be solved.

He discussed his crime with Hawkins, and said again that he

regretted deeply having betrayed his friends at Harwell and, in particular, Henry Arnold. He said nothing about any other betrayal.

After Fuchs had served some years, Hawkins asked him what he intended to do when he got out. Fuchs said he could not stay in Britain now that his British nationality had been taken away. (This was not necessarily so.) He said he did not want to go to a country in the Communist bloc, and in any case he could not. 'I couldn't go east of the Iron Curtain because over there I'm regarded as being largely responsible for the arrest of Harry Gold and David Greenglass, and for the execution of the Rosenbergs,' he explained.

He noted that Alan Nunn May had gone to teach at the University of Ghana after he was released from prison, and that J. B. S. Haldane, a leading British biologist and long-time Communist who had recently broken with Communism, had gone to India. The idea of going to the Third World appealed to him. 'I think I'll go to India,' he told Hawkins. 'There, I could do useful work, and they are neutral in the East — West conflict, which is where I stand.'

But this is not what he did. We can trace through Fuchs's own words the path that led away from his belief in Communism and his service in its cause. The path that took him back to Communism and service to the Communist Party once again, and to East Germany, is buried out of sight.

It may be important that he never worked out his regret for what he had done and his distaste for the state of mind that had inspired him in political terms. The nearest he got was a rejection of all political ideology: 'Blame me, and if you can't do that, blame Hitler and Karl Marx and Stalin and all their blasted company,' he had written to Arnold. For someone who is not ready for despairing resignation or the detachment of a Candide, and who needs a coherent view of society, 'a plague on all your houses' is not a satisfactory stance. It may be relevant that his father came and visited him twice in prison in Britain, and told him that he would like him to come to East Germany, and he would be allowed to do so. Also, he may have felt suddenly the need for a homeland.

Under British prison regulations, a prisoner who does not get into any trouble in prison or offend against the regulations is entitled to remission of one-third of his sentence for good conduct. Fuchs satisfied these conditions, and so he served only nine years and four months.

Shortly before his sentence came to an end, Peierls wrote to him offering to help him find a job in England, but he received no reply. Arnold visited him in Wakefield, at the request of MI5, and offered to help him sort out any financial affairs. Fuchs told him how hurt he was at being deprived of his British citizenship. He said he would have liked to remain in England, but now he would probably go to East Germany. He said he was still a confirmed Marxist. He said he thought that in East Germany, government officials often attained their positions because of their standing in the Communist Party rather than their ability, and this was wrong. He wanted the intelligentsia to have more voice in Government affairs in East Germany, and he wanted to lead a campaign to ensure that they did. This was the old Fuchs, who was going to tell the Soviet leaders what was wrong with their system.

Fuchs left Wakefield Prison on 23 June 1959. The prison authorities and the police are permitted, in exceptional circumstances, to facilitate a prisoner's journey to wherever he wants to go to start a new life. A police car drove Fuchs straight from prison to Heathrow Airport, where he boarded a Polish airliner for East Berlin. An Associated Press reporter got on the plane. Fuchs told him: 'I wish to say that I bear no resentment against Britain or any Western country for what has happened.' Again, this sounded like the old Fuchs, and the old arrogance. He felt that it was for him to display or dispense with resentment.

He was met at the airport in East Berlin by Klaus Kittowsky, who was now a university student, and they drove together to see his father. Then he went to a health resort for a rest. He had money in the bank in England, which he presumably transferred.

Fuchs was not a Philby or a Maclean, a spy coming in from the cold. His world was that of science, and this was the world to which he returned. He was offered, and accepted, the post of Deputy Director of the Institute of Nuclear Research at Rossendorf, a small town in pleasant wooded countryside near Dresden. He was also to lecture at the Akademie der Wissenschaften, an academic institute in Dresden.

He applied for membership in the German Communist Party, and was accepted. He married now, a woman who had been a student at Kiel University with him, Margaret Keilson. She also was a Communist Party member. Despite this apparent orthodoxy, it is noteworthy that although Fuchs has often travelled to other countries in the Communist bloc since he went to East Germany, he has never travelled to any country outside the bloc. Presumably, the authorities do not trust him sufficiently to allow him to go.

He did not contact any of his former friends in Britain or America. He wrote once to a former colleague at Harwell who was junior to him, Brian Flowers (now Lord Flowers), inviting him to a scientific conference he was organizing. It was a formal letter that did not acknowledge in any way that they had been acquainted: he addressed Flowers, whom he had always known as 'Brian', as 'Dr Flowers'. Flowers wrote back a brief letter addressed to 'Dear Klaus' and turning down the invitation. However, Fuchs did write to Gordon Hawkins, the assistant governor of Wakefield Prison, telling him: 'The conversations I had with you — in particular the philosophical ones — belong to the pleasant memories of my time at Wakefield.'

(Odd that he should have pleasant memories of Wakefield gaol.)

Soon after Fuchs went to East Germany, Nicholas Kurd found himself in West Berlin. He noticed that there was a conference in East Berlin which he thought Fuchs would probably be attending, ascertained that he would be there, and telephoned him; Fuchs suggested lunch, and Kurd crossed the Wall to meet him.

Fuchs told him over lunch that he was upset by the attitude of his friends in England; he thought they might have been more sympathetic. He said he knew how they felt, he understood that what he had done was wrong from their points of view, but there were mitigating circumstances, and they might have been more understanding of *his* point of view. He said the one person who had remained a good friend throughout his difficult times was Henry Arnold, and he asked to be remembered to him.

They touched on politics only once. Kurd said he had been reading the East German newspapers, and found them so narrowly one-sided in their view of events that they made the British Communist Party newspaper, the *Daily Worker,* seem like an organ of liberal opinion by comparison. Fuchs laughed at this and nodded sympathetically, but said that the Government in East Germany was trying to change society, and this was not easy.

The Director of the Institute for Nuclear Research was Heinz Barwich, a German physicist with pro-Soviet sympathies who had gone to the Soviet Union after the war and worked on the Soviet atomic bomb programme, and earned a Stalin Prize. At the Institute, Barwich had his difficulties with the Communist Party. A party bureaucrat was installed at the Institute and interfered with the way it was run, until Barwich found the situation intolerable and demanded his removal; after a struggle, he got it. When he learned that Fuchs was to join the

Institute as his deputy, he looked forward to having at his side a man who, as he saw it, had already shown great moral courage and independence. He assumed that Fuchs would be an ally in any future struggles with the bureaucracy. But he was disappointed; he found that Fuchs followed the Party line on everything dogmatically, and never differed from its dictates or its officials.

Barwich became disillusioned with Communism, and in 1964 he defected to the West while he was attending a scientific conference in Geneva. Later, he testified before a US congressional committee about the Soviet atomic bomb programme, and said that Fuchs, by his help, had probably saved the Russians two years' work.

On Fuchs's behaviour in East Germany, he recalled Fuchs's self-analytical confession that was read out at his trial, and the passages about dividing his mind into two compartments. He said that as he saw it, Fuchs had evidently decided to put an end to the split in his personality, and deliver himself totally to the service of Communism.

Certainly Fuchs had become, in his public persona at least, a dogmatically faithful Communist, following the party line on every issue, a transformation wrought by some combination of political reconversion, self-delusion and perhaps opportunism, for he had to live in East Germany and pursue his career there. He occasionally gave interviews to the official media supporting the official Soviet line on some issue of the day concerning nuclear weapons. When the Soviet Union ended its moratorium on nuclear weapons testing in 1961, he told the East German news agency that this was a correct and necessary step. In his only interview with a British newspaper, the *Daily Express,* he accused West Germany of setting out to build an atomic bomb.

In August 1986, when the Soviet Union was pressing the United States to sign a nuclear test ban to include underground tests, he wrote an article in *Neues Deutschland,* the official Communist Party newspaper, appealing for a worldwide ban on nuclear tests. 'The history of humanity cannot be allowed to end in an atomic inferno,' he wrote. 'I appeal to all men of goodwill who care about the future of our planet. Let us stand up for a ban on all nuclear weapons tests.'

He attended a colloquium held in East Berlin to mark the seventy-fifth anniversary of Max Planck's first paper on quantum theory. He presented a paper on the philosophical implications of the theory, although largely to dismiss them, in strict Marxist materialist terms. Underlining his orthodoxy, he quoted Marx in his paper: 'The question of whether human thought is capable of objective truth is not a question of theory but a practical question.' And he quoted Lenin: 'There is no abstract truth; truth is always concrete.' Coincidentally, another paper at this colloquium was read by Bruno Pontecorvo, who defected from Harwell the year after Fuchs was arrested and was given a post at a nuclear research institute near Moscow.

Fuchs was honoured in East Germany both for his scientific and his political work, although no reference was ever made to his espionage on behalf of the Communist cause. He was elected to the German Democratic Republic's Academy of Sciences, and also to the Communist Party Central Committee. He was awarded the Order of Merit of the Fatherland, and the Order of Karl Marx. On his seventieth birthday, the East German Communist leader, Erich Honneker, sent him a message saying: 'You can look back on a successful career as a Communist, a scientist and a university teacher.'

When Victor Weisskopf went to East Germany to give some lectures, he told scientists he met there that he would like to see Fuchs. Weisskopf has been deeply concerned with the moral and political implications of the manufacture of nuclear weapons ever since Los Alamos, and has often been critical of American policies. Fuchs telephoned him and invited him to lunch at a smart restaurant.

They talked about politics. Weisskopf criticized the Soviet Union on a number of issues: civil rights, Afghanistan, the treatment of Jews. Fuchs defended the Soviet Union all the way, but as always he spoke quietly and without passion. He would say to Weisskopf, mildly, 'No, I'm afraid you don't understand the situation,' or 'I don't think you're right about that.'

Weisskopf raised the treatment of Andrei Sakharov, the dissident Soviet physicist, and Fuchs became unexpectedly vehement, although he still spoke quietly. 'Sakharov is a traitor,' he said. 'He wants the United States to have more missiles than the Soviet Union. The Soviet authorities are treating him very well. These people deserve a harsher punishment.'

Fuchs's father lived for many more years to enjoy his son's success and prestige in his own country. He died in 1971, at the age of ninety-six. He wrote his autobiography, which was published in two slender volumes. He told an English friend that there was a third volume in manuscript form, which was to be published only after his death. 'I am not altogether popular with the authorities,' he explained with a twinkle. The manuscript has never been found.

Fuchs's sister in America, Kristel Heineman, recovered from her illness, married a second time and had three more children. Among others involved in Fuchs's story, Harry Gold was sentenced to thirty years' imprisonment for his role as a courier. He was brought out of prison to give evidence at the Rosenbergs' trial, and also at the trial of his former boss, Abraham Brothman, who was said to have passed secrets to Soviet agents. He was paroled in 1966, and died of heart disease in Philadelphia in 1972. Sir Rudolf Peierls moved to New College, Oxford, in 1963 and retired in 1974, and is now Professor Emeritus at Oxford University and the University of

Washington in Seattle; at the time of writing he still travels widely. Lady Peierls accompanied him on his travels, until she died of a brain disease in October 1987. Sir Nevill Mott was awarded the Nobel Prize for Physics in 1977. Herbert Skinner died in 1960 at the age of fifty-nine; his wife Erna died in 1975, of an asthma attack, at a gathering in the home of a friend from Harwell days. Henry Arnold retired from Harwell and went to live in the seaside town of Sandbanks, and died there at the age of eighty-eight. William Skardon retired to Torquay, and died there in 1988; MI5 had refused to allow him to write his memoirs.

Hans Bethe earned a Nobel Prize in Physics in 1967; his younger colleague, Richard Feynman, was awarded one two years earlier. Otto Frisch died in 1981. Klaus Kittowsky added his grandfather's name to his own and became Fuchs-Kittowsky, and followed an academic career; he is now a Professor of Information Technology at the Humboldt University in East Berlin. Igor Kurchatov, hailed as 'the father of the Soviet atomic bomb', died in 1960 at the age of fifty-seven, heaped with honours — Stalin Prize, Order of Lenin, member of the Soviet Parliament. Jurgen Kuczynksi lives in retirement in East Berlin; he recently confirmed for a West German television team his role in putting Fuchs in contact with Soviet agents.

Fuchs retired in 1979. He remained in good health for some years, although he was even thinner than he had been, almost gaunt, and was balding. He devoted a lot of his time to the officially sponsored peace movement. This always follows the Party line, but it would be simplistic to dismiss all its participants as nothing more than puppets. Most of them have chosen the area in which they wish to express their concern, and this was Fuchs's choice. He gave a number of lectures urging progress towards nuclear disarmament.

When the Soviet Congress of Scientists held a conference in 1983 in Moscow to discuss the prevention of nuclear war,

Fuchs was invited as a guest speaker. Another guest invited from abroad was Josef Rotblat, one of the heads of the Pugwash Movement, founded to join scientists of the world in working against nuclear war, and Rotblat found himself sitting next to Fuchs. It was some time before he recognized him; he had not seen him since Los Alamos days, and he did not know him very well there. Fuchs, in his talk to the conference, recalled Niels Bohr's letters to Roosevelt and Churchill pointing out the dangers of the nuclear arms race. Adhering always to Soviet orthodoxy, he also quoted Lenin, and denounced the SDI, the United States 'star wars' anti-missile defence programme.

Fuchs died suddenly, on 28 January, 1988, a month after his seventy-seventh birthday. The official announcement did not give the cause of his death.

The East German Press carried tributes to his work as a scientist and a political activist, but did not mention his espionage activities. ADN, the official East German news agency, carried a fulsome obituary, saying:

> 'His scientific achievements in the field of theoretical physics and his consistent actions for Socialism and the maintenance of peace have brought him high national and international esteem.
> 'As a Socialist scientist, university teacher, Communist and loyal friend of the Soviet Union, he participated for two decades, successfully and creatively, in the development of the power industry'

East German newspaper readers, unless they had other sources of information, would have no idea of Fuchs's principal contribution to the Communist cause.

Acknowledgment of this came six months later, in a Soviet television documentary about the Soviet atomic bomb programme shown during the first full flowering of *glasnost*.

Fuchs featured prominently in this film. It showed his

participation in the wartime atomic bomb programme in America and said: 'Fuchs knew that the bomb was a secret from Russia. He did not think this was right, and he gave data about the bomb to the Russians.' It also showed footage of Fuchs in East Germany, reading a British newspaper, and said that up until the time he died, he never repented what it called his 'awesome choice'. As we know, the truth is more complex.

Fuchs enjoyed an active retirement in his last years. He spent some time at the Akademie der Wissenschaften in Dresden, working on its archives. Visiting scientists would occasionally see him there.

A French scientist visiting an East German university made a detour to call in at the Akademie, travelling by car. He met a number of scientists there, including Fuchs. Chatting with Fuchs about his trip, he said the detour had delayed him, so that the one-week permit he was given for his car would expire before he returned. However, he said, it would be a lot of trouble to renew it for two days more, and he did not think he would bother; probably, nobody would notice.

Fuchs took a firm, disapproving line. 'I think,' he said, 'that if you are in another country, you should obey its laws.'

APPENDIX: KLAUS FUCHS'S CONFESSION

War Office, 27 January 1950

Statement of Emil Julius Klaus Fuchs, of 17 Hillside, Harwell, Berkshire, who said:

I am Deputy Chief Scientific Officer (acting rank) at Atomic Energy Research Establishment, Harwell.

I was born in Rüsselsheim on 29 December 1911. My father was a parson and I had a very happy childhood. I think that the one thing that mostly stands out is that my father always did what he believed to be the right thing to do and he always told us that we had to go our own way, even if he disagreed. He himself had many fights because he did what his conscience decreed, even if these were at variance with accepted convention. For example, he was the first parson to join the Social Democratic Party. I didn't take much interest in politics during my school days except in so far as I was forced into it by the fact that of course all the other pupils knew who my father was, and I think the only political act at school which I ever made was at the celebration of the Weimar Constitution when there was a celebration at school and all the flags of the Weimar Republic had been put up outside, whereas inside large numbers of the pupils appeared with the imperial badge. At that point I took out the badge showing the colours of the Republic, and put it on, and of course it was immediately torn down.

When I got to the University of Leipzig I joined the SPD and took part in the organization of the students' group of the SPD. I found myself soon in opposition to the official policies of the SPD, for example on the question of naval re-armament, when the SPD supported the building programme of the Panzercreuzer. I did have some discussion with Communists, but I always found that I despised them because it was apparent that they accepted the official policy of their own party even if they did not agree with it. The main point at issue was always the Communist policy proclaiming the united front and at the same time attacking the leaders of the SPD. Later I went to Kiel University. It has just occurred to me, though it may not be important, that at Leipzig I was in the Reichsbanner which was a semi-military organization composed of members of the SPD and the Democratic Party. That is a point at which I broke away from my father's philosophy because he is a pacifist. In Kiel I was first still a member of the SPD, but the break came when the SPD decided to support Hindenburg as Reich President. Their argument was that if they put up their own candidate it would split the vote and Hitler would be elected. In particular, this would mean that the position of the SPD in Prussia would be lost when they controlled the whole of the police organization. The election was, I think, in 1932. My argument was that we could not stop Hitler by co-operating with other bourgeois parties but that only a united working class could stop him. At this point I decided to oppose the official policies openly, and I offered myself as a speaker in support of the Communist candidate. Shortly after the election of Hindenburg, Papen was made Reich Chancellor, and he dismissed the elected Prussian Government and put in a Reichstathalter. That evening we all collected spontaneously. I went to the headquarters of the Communist Party because I had in the meantime been expelled from the SPD, but I had seen many of my previous friends in the Reichsbanner, and I knew that they were gathering together ready to fight for the Prussian Government, but the Prussian Government yielded. All they did was to appeal to the central Reich Court. At this point the morale of the rank and file of the SPD and the Reichsbanner broke completely and it was evident that there was no force left in those organizations to resist Hitler. I accepted that the Communist Party had been right in fighting against the leaders of the SPD and that I had been wrong in blaming them for it. I had already joined the Communist Party because I felt I had to be in some organization.

Some time before this I had also joined a student organization which contained members of the SPD, as well as members of the Communist Party. This organization was frowned upon by the SPD, but they did not take steps against me until I came out openly against the official policy. I was made the Chairman of this organization and we carried on propaganda aimed at those members of the Nazi Party whom we believed to be sincere. The Nazis had decided to start propaganda against the high fees which students had to pay, and we decided to take them by their word, convinced that we would show them up. I carried on the negotiations with the leaders of the Nazi group at the University, proposing that we should organize a strike of the students. They hedged and after several weeks I decided that the time had come to show that they did not intend to do it. We issued a leaflet, explained that the negotiations had been going on but that the leaders of the Nazis were not in earnest. Our policy did have success because some members of our organization succeeded in making personal contact with some of the sincere Nazis. The Nazi leaders apparently noticed that, because some time later they organized a strike against the Rector of the University. That was after Hitler had been made Reich Chancellor. During that strike they called in the support of the SA from the town, who demonstrated in front of the University. In spite of that I went there every day to show that I was not afraid of them. On one of these occasions they tried to kill me and I escaped. The fact that Hindenburg made Hitler Reich Chancellor of course proved to me again that I had been right in opposing the official policy of the SPD. After the burning of the Reichstag I had to go underground. I was lucky because on the morning after the burning of the Reichstag I left my home very early to catch a train to Berlin for a conference of our student organization, and that is the only reason why I escaped arrest. I remember clearly when I opened the newspaper in the train I immediately realized the significance and I knew that the underground struggle had started. I took the badge of the hammer and sickle from my lapel which I had carried until that time.

I was ready to accept the philosophy that the Party is right and that in the coming struggle you could not permit yourself any doubts after the Party had made a decision. At this point I omitted from resolve in my mind a very small difficulty about my conduct of the policy against the Nazis. I received, of course, a great deal of praise at the conference in Berlin which was held illegally, but there rankled in my mind the fact that I had sprung our leaflets on the leaders of the Nazis without warning, without giving them an ultimatum that I would call to the student body lest they made a decision by a certain date. If it had been necessary to do that I would not have worried about it, but there was no need for it. I had violated some standards of decent behaviour, but I did not resolve this difficulty and very often this incident did come back to my mind, but I came to accept that in such a struggle of things of this kind are prejudices which are weakness and which you must fight against.

All that followed helped to confirm the ideas I had formed. Not a single party voted against the extraordinary powers which were given to Hitler by the new Reichstag and in the universities there was hardly anybody who stood up for those who were dismissed on either political or racial grounds, and afterwards you found that people whom you normally would have respected because of their decency had no force in themselves to stand up for their own ideals or moral standards.

I was in the underground until I left Germany. I was sent out by the Party, because they said that I must finish my studies because after the revolution in Germany people would be required with technical knowledge to take part in the building up of the Communist Germany. I went first to France and then to England, where I studied and at the same time I tried to make a serious study of the base Marxist philosophy. The idea which gripped me most was the belief that in the past man has been unable to understand his own history and the forces which lead to the further development of human society; that now for the first time man understands the historical forces and he is able to control them, and that, therefore, for the first time he will be really free. I carried this idea over into the personal sphere and believed that I could understand myself and that I could make myself into what I believed I should be.

I accepted for a long time that what you heard about Russia internally could be deliberate lies. I had my doubts for the first time on acts of foreign policies of Russia; the Russo-German pact was difficult to understand, but in the end I did accept that Russia had done it to gain time, that during that time she was expanding her own influence in the Balkans against the influence of Germany. Finally Germany's attack on Russia seemed to confirm that Russia was not shirking and was prepared to carry out a foreign policy with the risk of war with Germany. Russia's attack on Finland was more difficult to understand, but the fact that England and France prepared for an intervention in Finland at the time when they did not appear to be fighting seriously against Germany made it possible to accept the explanation that Russia had to prepare its defences against possible imperialist powers. In the end I accepted again that my doubts had been wrong and the Party had been right.

When Germany started the real attack on France I was interned and for a long time I was not allowed any newspapers. We did not know what was going on outside, and I did not see how the British people fought at that time. I felt no bitterness at the internment, because I could understand that it was necessary and that at that time England could not spare good people to look after the internees, but it did deprive me of the chance of learning more about the real character of the British people.

Shortly after my release I was asked to help Professor Peierls in Birmingham, on some war work. I accepted it and I started work without knowing at first what the work was. I doubt whether it would have made any difference to my subsequent actions if I had known the nature of the work beforehand.

When I learned the purpose of the work I decided to inform Russia and I established contact through another member of the Communist Party. Since that time I have had continuous contact with persons who were completely unknown to me, except that I knew that they would hand whatever information I gave them to the Russian authorities. At this time I had a complete confidence in Russian policy and I believed that the Western Allies deliberately allowed Russia and Germany to fight each other to the death. I had, therefore, no hesitation in giving all the information I had, even though occasionally I tried to concentrate mainly on giving information about the results of my own work.

In the course of this work I began naturally to form bonds of personal friendship and I had concerning them my inner thoughts. I used my Marxist philosophy to establish in my mind two separate compartments. One compartment in which I allowed myself to make friendships, to have personal relations, to help people and to be in all personal ways the kind of man I wanted to be and the kind of man which, in personal ways, I had been before with my friends in or near the Communist Party. I could be free and easy and happy with other people without fear of disclosing myself because I knew that the other compartment would step in if I approached the danger point. I could forget the other compartment and still rely on it. It appeared to me at the time that I had become a 'free man' because I had succeeded in the other compartment to establish myself completely independent of the surrounding forces of society. Looking back at it now the best way of expressing it seems to be to call it a controlled schizophrenia.

In the postwar period I began again to have my doubts about Russian policy. It is impossible to give definite incidents because now the control mechanism acted against me, also keeping away from me facts which I could not look in the face, but they did penetrate and eventually I came to a point when I knew I disapproved of a great many actions of the Russian Government and of the Communist Party, but I still believed that they would build a new world and that one day I would take part in it and that on that day I would also have to stand up and say to them that there are things which they are doing wrong. During this time I was not sure that I could give all the information that I had. However, it became more and more evident that the time when Russia would expand her influence over Europe was far away, and that, therefore, I had to decide for myself whether I could go on for many years to continue handing over information without being sure in my own mind whether I was doing right. I decided that I could not do so. I did not go to one rendezvous because I was ill at the time. I decided not to go to the following one.

Shortly afterwards my father told me that he might be going into the Eastern Zone of Germany. At that time my own mind was closer to his than it had ever been before, because he also believed that they are at least trying to build a new world. He disapproved of many things and he had always done so, but he knew that when he went there he would say so and he thought that in doing so he might help to make them realize that you cannot build a new world if you destroy some fundamental decencies in personal behaviour. I could not bring myself to stop my father from going there. However, it made me face at last some of the facts about myself. I felt that my father's going to the Eastern Zone, that his letters, would touch me somewhere and that I was not sure whether I would not go back. I suppose I did not have the courage to fight it out for myself and, therefore, I invoked an outside influence by informing Security that my father was going to the Eastern Zone. A few months passed and I became more and more convinced that I had to leave Harwell. I was then confronted with the fact that there was evidence that I had given away information in New York. I was given the chance of admitting it and staying at Harwell, or of clearing out. I was not sure enough of myself to stay at Harwell and, therefore, I denied the allegations and decided that I would have to leave Harwell.

However, it then began to become clear to me that in leaving

Harwell in those circumstances I would do two things. I would deal a grave blow to Harwell, to all the work which I had loved and, furthermore, that I would leave suspicions against people whom I loved who were my friends and who believed I was their friend. I had to face the fact that it had been possible for me in one half of my mind to be friendly with people, be close friends and at the same time to deceive them, to endanger them. I had to realize that the control mechanism had warned me of danger to myself, but that it had also prevented me from realizing what I was doing to people who were close to me. I then realized that the combination of the three ideas which had made me what I was, was wrong, in fact that every single one of them was wrong, that there are certain standards of moral behaviour which are in you and that you cannot disregard. That in your actions you must be clear in your own mind whether they are right or wrong. That you must be able, before accepting somebody else's authority, to state your doubts and to try and resolve them; and I found at least I myself was made by circumstances.

I know that I cannot go back on that and I know that all I can do now is to try and repair the damage I have done. The first thing is to make sure that Harwell will suffer as little as possible and that I have to save for my friends as much as possible of that part that was good in my relations with them.

This thought is at present uppermost in my mind, and I find it difficult to concentrate on any other points. However, I realize that I will have to state the extent of the information that I have given and that I shall have to help as far as my conscience allows me in stopping other people who are still doing what I have done.

There is nobody I know by name who is concerned with collecting information for the Russian authorities. There are people whom I know by sight whom I trusted with my life and who trusted me with theirs and I do not know that I shall be able to do anything that might in the end give them away.

They are not inside of the project, but they are the intermediaries between myself and the Russian Government.

At first I thought that all I would do would be to inform the Russian authorities that work upon the atom bomb was going on. They wished to have more details and I agreed to supply them. I concentrated at first mainly on the products of my own work, but in particular at Los Alamos I did what I consider to be the worst I have done, namely to give information about the principles of the design of the plutonium bomb. Later on at Harwell I began to sift it, but it is difficult to say exactly when and how I did it because it was a process which went up and down with my inner struggles. The last time I handed over information was in February or March, 1949.

Before I joined the project most of the English people with whom I had made personal contacts were left-wing, and affected, to some degree or other, by the same kind of philosophy. Since coming to Harwell I have met English people of all kinds, and I have come to see in many of them a deep-rooted firmness which enables them to lead a decent way of life. I do not know where this springs from and I don't think they do, but it is there.

I have read this statement and to the best of my knowledge it is true.

(signed) Klaus Fuchs
Statement taken down in writing by me at the permission of Emil Julius Klaus Fuchs at the War Office on January 27, 1950. He read it through, made such alterations as he wished and initialled each and every page.

(signed) W. J. Skardon

Acknowledgements

I am grateful to the following people for providing me with information about Klaus Fuchs or his background. They are listed here according to the place of their principal association with Fuchs, although in many cases they knew him at other stages of his career as well.

For convenience, I am leaving out the academic titles of 'Doctor' and 'Professor' since the majority of people on this list have them. A few other informants have preferred to remain anonymous.

Bristol University

John Burrow, Harry Jones, Sir Bernard Lovell, Sir Nevill Mott, Norman Thompson

Camp Sherbrooke

Heinz Arndt, Sir Herman Bondi, Gerard Friedlander, Erich Koch, Anthony Michaelis, Paul Streeten

Los Alamos

Luis Alvarez, Harold and Mary Argo, Hans Bethe, Norris Bradbury, Mrs Hannah Bretscher, Bernice Brode, David Brode, Martin and Suzanne Deutsch, John de Wire, Bernard Feld, Richard Feynman, A. P. French, Roy Glauber, Edwin and Elsie McMillan, John Manley, Carson and Kathleen Mark, Robert and Ruth Marshak, Nicholas Metropolis, Josef Rotblat, Cyril and Alice Smith, Rod Spence, Edward Teller, Victor and Ellen Weisskopf, Robert and Jane Wilson

Harwell

Joy Alexander, Henry Arnold,[xxvii] Oscar Buneman, Fred Fenning, Lord and Lady Flowers, Otto Frisch,[xxviii] Mrs Ursula Frisch, James Hill, Alwyn McKay, A. G. Maddock, Sir Michael Perrin, Terence Price, Compton and Marjorie Rennie, Hugh and Jill Roskell, Mrs Eleanor Scott, Henry Seligman, William Skardon, Mrs Erna Skinner[1] John and Marjorie Storey, John Tait, Mrs Elaine Wheatley (formerly Elaine Skinner)

Other and general

Margaret Gowing, Mrs Gaby Gross (formerly Gaby Peierls), Gordon Hawkins, David Holloway, Nicholas Kurti, Ted Milligan, Sir Rudolf and Lady Peierls.

Notes

Much of the information in this book comes from interviews with people who knew Klaus Fuchs at various stages of his career, in some cases several extensive interviews with the same person. These people are listed in the Acknowledgements section.

I first became interested in Fuchs some years ago when I was doing research on some aspects of nuclear weapons, and his name came up in conversations with some people who knew him, and I looked up the details of the case. Then I did a radio programme about him which was broadcast in 1976, in which five people who knew him took part: Henry Arnold, Nicholas Kurd, Sir Rudolf and Lady Peierls, and Mrs Erna Skinner. This was broadcast by the Canadian Broadcasting Corporation and the BBC. So I had material to draw on when I began doing researches for this book.

Much of the documentary source material comes from FBI files, although much of this originates in Britain. It was obtained under the Freedom of Information Act. British official papers are normally made available to the public after thirty years, but it was announced at the end of 1979 that the papers relating to the Fuchs case would not be released because of what were said to be security considerations. None the less, a small amount of material was available among official papers of the Foreign Office and the atomic energy programme.

The most important single documents from the FBI files are:

> The full text of Fuchs's formal confession, which is printed in the Appendix. The British authorities sent this to the FBI, and it is in the files because the then FBI Director, J. Edgar Hoover, sent it in a letter to Rear Admiral Sidney W. Souers, a Special Consultant to President Truman.

A lengthy account of Fuchs's interviews with FBI agents in Wormwood Scrubs prison, in which he went over details of his espionage activities. Since he was very forthcoming to British intelligence officers, he presumably told these everything he told the FBI men, but no reports of these interviews are available.

Sir Michael Perrin's report of Fuchs's account to him of what he told the Russians.

Harry Gold's confession. I have treated this with caution because of Gold's record as a fantasist, but everything in it conforms with Fuchs's own account, apart from one or two minor points that could easily be due to a slip of the memory on the part of one or the other with the lapse of years, and it adds some details.

I also drew on reports of FBI agents' interviews and letters that were in the FBI files.

I wrote to Fuchs himself a number of times requesting an interview and information, and an intermediary made the same request on my behalf. His only response was to send me a copy of his address to the Moscow meeting of the All-Union Congress of Scientists on Preventing Nuclear War.

Most of the accounts of Fuchs's behaviour come from more than one source. In most of the notes that follow, I have indicated the source or sources. Where none is indicated, it is either because it is obvious from the context, or because the sources were too many and diffuse to record, or else because it is a matter of public record (e.g. a trial in open court).

here.

End Notes

Chapter One

[i] Arthur Koestler, Arrow in the Blue.

[ii] This is unfair. When the Enabling Act to give extraordinary powers to Hitler came up in the Reichstag, some Socialists were under arrest, but eighty-four attended and voted against the Act, despite browbeating and threats by the Nazis.

[iii] See, for instance, the important book The Origins of Totalitarian Democracy by J. L. Talmon. Talmon argues that the fundamental political conflict in our time is between liberal and what he calls totalitarian democracy.

Chapter Two

[iv] In those days spies were not respectable, and no countries admitted employing them. These are more frank and permissive times, and Ruth Kuczynski, now living in well-earned retirement in East Germany, was allowed to publish her memoirs, as well as some fictional spy thrillers. Her memoirs do not say she was Fuchs's contact, but this can easily be deduced from them. See the notes at the end of this book.

[v] From 'The Soviet Decision to Build the Atomic Bomb, 1939-45', in Social Studies of Science, 1981.

[vi] I was at a boarding school in New York, and I remember well us all being taught in chapel to sing the rousing Cossack Song. — NM

[vii] Fuchs was using the word 'schizophrenia' in a way that it is used often, and inaccurately, by laymen, to mean a division into two distinct personalities, Dr Jekyll and Mr Hyde being the classic example. Used correctly, it means a psychotic disorder involving complete emotional disorientation.

Chapter Three

[viii] Teller played a crucial role in the invention of the hydrogen bomb in 1951.

[ix] Harry S. Truman, 1945: Year of Decisions.

[x] G. K. Zhukov, Reminiscences and Reflections. This passage is quoted and translated by David Holloway in The Soviet Union and the Arms Race.

Chapter Four

[xi] County boundaries have been changed, and today Harwell is in Oxfordshire.

[xii] Margaret Gowing, *Independence and Deterrence: Britain and Atomic Energy, 1945-52.*

[xiii] As I have written elsewhere, that phrase 'including atomic weapons' must be one of the great throwaway lines of British history. — NM

[xiv] In a radio interview with me for a programme about Klaus Fuchs, broadcast by the BBC on 1 August 1977. — NM

[xv] This is told in Ignotus's autobiographical book Political Prisoner.

[xvi] Behan recalled this episode in a record of talk and songs.

[xvii] This was what the original announcement of the Hiroshima bomb said was its power. Subsequent analysis showed it to be about thirteen kilotons.

Chapter Five

[xviii] See Peter Wright's book about MI5, Spycatcher.

[xix] Certainly the case cast a shadow of doubt over the foreign-born scientists who had done secret war work. The wife of one of these said years later, 'I must admit I was secretly pleased when Burgess and Maclean and Philby turned out to be spies. They were not foreign, they were not Jewish, they were true-blue British and had been to the best schools and to Cambridge.'

Chapter Six

[xx] I obtained a copy of the full confession from the FBI files in Washington DC, and used it as source material. It is reprinted in the Appendix. This is the first time it has been published in Britain. — NM

[xxi] Dean Acheson, Present at the Creation^ Norton, New York, 1969.

[xxii] This must have been a mistake. She visited him in Brixton but not in Wormwood Scrubs.

[xxiii] Portal, as Viscount Portal of Hungerford, became head of the atomic energy programme after the war; he told this story to another official of the programme after Fuchs was sent to prison, and this official told it to me. — NM

[xxiv] Quoted in Robert Jungk, Brighter than a Thousand Suns.

[xxv] It is a plausible supposition. The Hungarian General Bela Kiraly, who commanded a Soviet Bloc army before he fled to the West after the Soviet invasion of Hungary in 1956, told an interviewer that Soviet acquisition of the atomic bomb allowed Russia to give North Korea the go-ahead to invade. 'It gave Stalin a kind of security that the Soviet Union was no longer a target which could not reciprocate in kind,' he said. See Michael Charlton, The Eagle and the Small Birds, BBC, London, 1984.

xxvi The Home Secretary, whose formal title is Secretary of State for Home Affairs.

Acknowledgements

xxvii 1 I interviewed Henry Arnold and Mrs Skinner for a radio programme about Fuchs that was broadcast in 1976 and 1977. Both died before I began my researches for this book.

xxviii Otto Frisch talked to me about Fuchs in a conversation some years ago, and I have drawn on this at one or two points. He died before I began this book.

Printed in Great Britain
by Amazon